Rowing Against the Tide

Martin M. Brandon-Bravo

www.BretwaldaBooks.com
@Bretwaldabooks
bretwaldabooks.blogspot.co.uk/
Bretwalda Books on Facebook

First Published 2013
Text nad Photos Copyright © Martin Brandon-Bravo 2013
Martin Brandon-Bravo asserts his moral rights to be regarded as the author
of this book.

Bretwalda Books
Unit 8, Fir Tree Close, Epsom,
Surrey KT17 3LD
info@BretwaldaBooks.com
www.BretwaldaBooks.com
ISBN 978-1-909698-03-1

Printed and bound in Great Britain by
Marston Book Services Limited, Oxfordshire

CONTENTS

To my wife Sally and my two sons Paul and Joel who at home ran what they called the Department of Realism

Prologue

Growing up in North London and the East End might not auger well for a successful and satisfying career, but whether by good luck or good fortune, I've had by any yardstick, an interesting life. Writing now at the age of eighty, I'm looking back in the knowledge that I cannot expect to be around for many more years. Three major cancer operations in 2010 was quite a wakeup call, particularly to someone who apart from breaking his nose three times, had hardly ever been ill.

So putting pen to paper, or rather tapping away on a lap-top, I look back on my childhood in Stoke Newington and Hammersmith, National Service in the Royal Artillery, thirty years in the manufacturing textile industry with overlapping forty years in Local and National Politics, plus a lifetime involved in the sport of Rowing.

Through forty eight of those years I've had the love and support of my wife Sally, the joy of two great sons, Paul and Joel, and the pleasure of wonderful grandchildren. I readily acknowledge that without Sally's support I doubt I would have made it to the House of Commons, and would not have had so successful a career in my sport which culminated in being elected President of the Amateur Rowing Association, now rebranded as British Rowing. In every aspect of my career, Sally has been there, prodding and encouraging me, and I owe her more thanks than I could ever repay.

Over those years, business, sport, and politics, have given me the chance to see the world, making friends and acquaintances across the globe, though sadly with many it's now only an exchange of Christmas Cards.

It was all topped off by the award in December 2001 of the OBE, for services to my sport, and nothing whatever to do with my life in politics. Retiring from Local Government in 2009, both the County and City of Nottinghamshire granted me the honour of Aldermanship, a more than satisfying way to end and put my feet up.

Martin B-B

Yours truly

CHAPTER 1

THE EARLY DAYS

Number 68 Belgrade Road Stoke Newington, North London, was a typical soundly built, comfortable, terraced house, but not perhaps the most auspicious of starting places for what turned out, fortuitously for me, to have been a varied and interesting life. I was born at No 3 but we moved to No 68 within weeks of my birth. I had an older brother Michael, and would have had an even older brother, who was always referred to as poor Harry boy, who died at the age of three with peritonitis. My mother and father were married in the first purpose built Synagogue in England, Bevis Marks, in St Mary le Bow near the Baltic exchange. At around 1650 Cromwell had in practical terms allowed us back into England after a four hundred year exclusion, but it was King Charles II who granted the newly approved return of the Jewish community to build that first synagogue. It's a record I cannot definitely confirm, but it is believed my family donated seven and sixpence to the fundraising at that time. The land was leased in 1698 and the Synagogue completed in 1703. Today it stands just as if time has stood still, and is a fascinating place to visit, with its wooden benches and chandeliers lit with real candles !

When we arrived in England has not been truly established, but as our name implies, we may have been kicked out from Spain in the expulsions of the late 1400s, and then from Portugal no later than 1595. The Brandon bit may have been Brandao in Spain, with both spellings found in Portugal, for always when we have holidayed there and presented our credit card, we have been greeted by – "ah so your Portuguese?", followed by my

"no, we left a few hundred years ago, and its too long a story" !
I've often said to enquiring friends that we may have been illegal
immigrants before then, but don't tell the Home Office.

We were not an overly practicing Jewish family, for strict
orthodoxy has never appealed, appearing to reject an ever
changing world, in a way that Reform or Progressive Judaism
has not done. Orthodoxy drew a line in the 1500s, and whilst
Reform Judaism revised and then drew the line in the late 1800s,
the Liberal and Progressive arm embraces new discoveries and
adapts its ways more in keeping with the rabbinic oral traditions
of biblical times. Never the less, my mother, Phoebe, kept a
reasonable kosher home, and only broke from that tradition
when the then Chief Rabbi gave dispensation as a result of the
shortages that the war and rationing brought in. But as time has
gone by, I have become ever more sceptical, noting that more
people have died in the name of the Lord than for any other
reason. I suppose I'm an agnostic, as indeed I find most, even
practicing members, of my faith are, for its true that 10 Jews in
a discussion will have 100 different views on every subject.

My father, Alf, who was eleven years old before he found his
name was really Isaac, was a master cabinet maker, and most of
the furniture in our home was built by him. The French polish
had a depth of gloss that no furniture cream was ever allowed,
or found necessary. It was a working class family, and so far as
I knew they always voted Labour, as indeed most immigrant or
minority communities did back then. In fact our end of London
had the only Communist MP, and oddly enough when we were
later effectively bombed out of the East End, we ended up in
Hammersmith with the only other English Communist member
D.N.Pritt MP

Just around the corner from Belgrave Rd was a small
synagogue on Walford Rd, but somehow I never felt comfortable
in what I found was an oppressive atmosphere. Our family being
of Sephardic origin never spoke a word of Yiddish which
perhaps added to my feeling of not quite belonging. Even so, our

best non family friends were the Gees, whose name I discovered later was originally Gonski, so clearly of Central European origin. They were a great family of three unmarried but sublimely happy spinsters, and two brothers, one a fishmonger on Stamford Hill, and the other the purser on the Empress of Britain. The sisters' great interest and activity covered, cards – mostly bridge – horse racing, and buying and selling shares. The latter activity bore little reference to the advice in financial papers, for they would only buy shares valued in pence (old money) and could therefore get a lot of shares for their modest outlay. When Butlins Holiday Camps took a knock when an overseas project did not work out, their shares crashed to around a dozen pence, and they bought, for them, quite a holding. I laughed and said that's no way to invest, but when those shares rose first to two and sixpence, I joined in for the ride, and as I recall we bailed out at over a pound a share. I never questioned my "aunts" investment policy again.

In those war years, and shortly after, when rationing was still in place, there were a few amusing anomalies, and one involving those "aunties". They always took my brother and me out for a treat on a date close to our birthdays, Michael's in February, and mine in March, and probably close to the war end, we were treated to supper in the West End at a restaurant called Iso's. At that time restaurants were only allowed to charge a maximum of five shillings (25 pence in today's money) per person, to meet rationing rules. However at this restaurant when you arrived you were asked, "How many are you?" We were five, but one of the sisters would say seven or eight, and the meal and the bill set accordingly. As ever there are always ways round the best of intentions in rules and regulations.

Some years later whilst umpiring at the Docklands Regatta in East London, I found myself chatting away with a distinguished Steward of the Royal Regatta, Fred Smallbone, who it turned out, had as a young boy, delivered fresh fish on his bicycle for my "uncle" Ernie Gee, whose shop was on Stamford Hill. Much to the consternation and puzzlement of two officials from London Rowing Club, our conversation rattled on about those old days, with my accent becoming more and more like Ken Livingstone by the minute.

Those seven years leading up to the second World War, were happy ones, for whilst we had nothing special, the only toys I recall were a three wheel bike, which at the age of about three I crashed into a garden wall and broke my nose for the first time of three. The other was a wondrous spinning top for a Christmas present – we celebrated everything – which I found at the bottom of my parents bed one Christmas morning.

I do recall the street party at the coronation of King George V1, and suffered the indignity of being dressed as some sort of clown. I remember too the Walls ice-cream vendor on his three wheeled bicycle coming round each week, and of course the coal merchant and his giant shire horse. Apparently there was a bit of a fallout with some neighbours, when my father first took a week's holiday with the family to Margate. Back then most could not afford such a holiday, and took objection to a family of Jews who could! One of those neighbours must have called my mother a f****** Jew, and she got a thumping from mums handbag, and mum was bound over to keep the peace by the local magistrate.

Sometime in those late 1930s, I had my first intimation of the sport of rowing. At the age of about six or seven, the Boat Race was getting its usual publicity. Any connection with North or the East End of London with our great Universities could not have been more remote, yet there were peddlers with their trays of light and dark blue ribbons, and everyone it seemed had to make their choice. My elder brother pulled rank and claimed Cambridge's colours, and imperiously told me I must therefore support Oxford. I don't think it really registered with me, but I duly wore a dark blue ribbon. As it turned out, I've continued to shout for the Dark Blues and just as well, since our youngest, Joel, made it to Oriel.

At that time too, I developed an interest in football, and as my father took me to Highbury for the first time at either six or seven years of age, I've followed the fortunes of the Gunners ever since. In fact, just as I suppose is the case in Glasgow, if you lived in that area of London, you chose either Arsenal or Spurs, or left town! More than seventy years on, I still get the wobbles until the football results are declared, and my day is complete when the Gunners have won, and joyous if the opponents are either Spurs or Chelsea. I went to Nottingham at the age of twenty, and joined the local Nottingham and Union Rowing Club. There were three rowing clubs adjacent to the Nottingham Forest ground, and just some ten or fifteen minutes into the second half, they used to open the gates on the riverside, and we would walk in for free to see the last thirty or so minutes of the game. Try as I could, I just could not work up any enthusiasm for Forest, for those childhood visits to Highbury had made me a "Gooner" for life.

I recall trying on gas masks in either '38 or '39, when the clouds of war were gathering, and the coaches that gathered at our school, Princess May Road, when we were supposed to be evacuated. As it happened when my brother and I had our labels tied on, my mother changed her mind and stated we would all stay together, and no official was going to shift her. The gas mask training came in handy many years later when in Israel with a small Parliamentary delegation led by the now Lord Greville Janner, during the first Gulf War.

In the late thirties we holidayed in Hove, staying with a couple of elderly ladies who owned a flat over a garage in Norton Place, close to the Hove Town Hall. Strangely my Parliamentary colleague Sir Ivan Lawrence QC, some four years my junior, lived just around the corner but this only came to light when reading his autobiography.

We were in Hove that September '39 where my brother and I used to delight in helping a guy called Hatton set out his beach huts. The police came down to the beach to tell us that War had been declared and we had to leave the beach at once. My brother Michael had wandered off towards Worthing, and my Mother was not going to leave that beach, Hitler or no Hitler, until he was found. The copper had met his match, and we returned to the flat only once Michael had been found. Dad decided we should stay put until things became clearer, and he travelled down each weekend after closing up the factory, which by that time he had become manager. Just before the phony War ended, we returned to London to stay with my grandmother in Grafton Street, just off the Mile End Road, and just in time for the first daylight raids on London. We'd built an Anderson shelter in her back garden, and Michael wielding a trenching shovel, broke my nose for its second time, leaving a deep cut between the eyes shedding blood making the damage look much worse than it was. I was rushed off to hospital, leaving my mother asking why the boy's mother had not come forward. Nobody had the nerve to tell her it was me. The night the docklands was hit and some sugar barges and warehouses caught fire, the flames could be seen for miles. That was when our family and neighbours came to the full realisation of what was to come in this war with Nazi Germany.

We had thought that the primary school I had attended in Brighton was a good school, but when back in the East End, I was sent to the Jewish Free School and found myself two years behind my age group. What I did not know at the time, was that I was mildly dyslectic and was just assumed as being slow, and maybe a bit thick, but what would now have been classed as one with special needs. We enjoyed collecting shrapnel and the bits of coloured marble from the wreck of a bombed building on the Mile End Road, but when the bombing became too intense, we climbed on the back of a sand lorry going to West London where we thought we would be safer ! My Aunt and Uncle Diana and Jack Davis, the latter being a director of Simpsons the tailoring manufacturers, lived on Emlyn Rd in Stamford Brook on the border between Hammersmith and Chiswick, and we slept on the floor for a few nights until dad found a house to rent in the adjoining Palgrave Road, and we stayed there throughout the blitz. The first Doodle Bug and the V2 landed in Chiswick not far from us, so any idea that it was safer, was distinctly marginal.

Dad had been in the Royal Flying Corps in WW1, cheating on his age to enable him to sign up. He flew the two man bombers, which had small bombs on hooks under the wings supposedly operated by a wire. If it didn't work you crawled out, detached it and flung it over the side. This we found out very much later, for like many from that terrible war, Dad just didn't want to talk about it, and from the films we've seen, I can quite understand.

I went to the Askew Road Primary in Shepherds Bush, and must have made some progress, for I passed the eleven plus, much to the astonishment of my family from whom I collected the princely sum of five pounds as a prize. My father had won a scholarship way back before WW1, but it was financially impossible for the family to let him take it up, and he was determined that his sons would not face that same disappointment.

When Russia came into the War, if you shopped at the Co-Op, which we rarely did, you could pass your dividend to aid for "Uncle Joe". If you weren't a Co-Op member, you could use a special number for the same purpose. The Co-Op organised an evening for us kids, with soft drinks and cake, which in the circumstances was great. However a few weeks later when they sought to repeat the exercise, we were treated to a political lecture, and that put an end to any lingering doubts I may have had. The idea of being brainwashed at nine years of age appalled me.

At the height of the blitz my father knocked up bunk beds under the stairs for my brother and me, which was known to be the safest place in a house. However it wasn't too long before we took the common view that if our names were on it, that would be it, and went back upstairs to bed. One night when the bombing had been very heavy, and a fair number had fallen nearby, my brother with his arm around me looked out in horror at a blaze just hidden behind the homes opposite. It turned out that a small shop kept by two elderly ladies had received a direct hit, killing both, and it now forms part of the land occupied by Queen Charlotte's Hospital on the Goldhawk Road.

At the time, many had been encouraged to install a steel Morrison Shelter in the home for families to sleep under, but we used instead a large, very robust, wooden table for use during the daylight doodle-bug raids. On one occasion when the engine stopped my mother was standing in the kitchen door on the opposite corner to the table under which Michael and I sheltered. As the engine note died, we shouted to mum who jumped from the kitchen door in one bound to under the table, and we were more incredulous of the length of the leap, than the crash of the plane barely fifty yards away to rear of our garden. We were sure it would have been a world record standing jump! Our windows had been blown out, and as the dust settled there was a knock on the front door and a white faced postman, asked if he could come in and sit down for a moment. He said that he had looked up when the doodle bug's engine had stopped, and thought it was going to spear him through, but somehow it lifted over our house and landed just behind us destroying houses on Emlyn Road where my aunt and uncle had lived.

There are countless stories of how civilians coped during those years of the Blitz, and dad who by then was too old to sign up, became an ARP warden and used to stand up against a single brick wall at the end of road. One night he heard a crash just behind him, for an incendiary bomb had landed on the top of the wall and fallen on the other side. It was a narrow escape by the width of a brick, and without thinking told my mother. It had been a very stressful week with the blitz, and she became hysterical. Dad had to slap her to bring her round, and she had a quiet sob in his arms as she recovered her composure. He'd done the right thing, and it was the first and only time he ever raised his hands to her. There had been a block of flats in Hammersmith that had received a direct hit, and during the rescue an old man was heard laughing and was found still in bed when he was rescued. His laughter was because he had been sleeping on the top floor, and was still in bed when found at ground level.

All of my generation will have stories of the war and its ending, but I will certainly never forget the joy and relief at the broadcast that the war in Europe was over. My father and I promptly went up to the West End of London and to the Marble Arch, where the scenes of jubilation were fantastic. The flat concrete roofed air-raid shelters provided ideal stages for dancing and public displays, and I recall servicemen stripped to the waist, cavorting around on top of one of these shelters close to the Arch. Where the food and booze had come from for those festivities was a secret I never discovered. One of those secrets was the appearance of chicken on restaurant and café menus. Today chicken is the most plentiful and cheapest of meats, back then it was a rare delicacy, but there it was at the announcement of peace in Europe mysteriously available to the celebrating crowd.

Like youngsters of my age, my pocket money had to be earned, and I delivered papers for a small newsagent, Nixons, on the Stamford Brook Rd. Latymer's headmaster did not approve of this kind of work before school, so I hid my school cap until the round was finished. He tried once more to raise the image of the school, by requesting that from the Fifth Form upwards, we should wear straw boaters. Too many pupils lived in Shepherds Bush, and after a few had their boaters trashed by the local lads, the scheme was scrapped.

At the War's end and still a slow reader, I absorbed the headlines, and I recall my bewilderment when seeing the headlines in 1945 – LABOUR LANDSLIDE. Winston Churchill by then was my idol, and even today I can listen to recordings of his speeches and experience the same emotion that they generated all those years ago. I just could not understand why he had been rejected, but looking back many years later I realised that many recalled how the "land fit for heroes" had not been fulfilled back in 1919, and the only alternative to the recognised Conservative establishment, was the Labour Party under Clement Attlee.

CHAPTER 2

SCHOOL DAYS

Those who had passed the eleven plus, had a few months at the nearby Secondary Modern School whilst waiting for the results of the entrance exams to the "Grammars" in West London. There were three, St Pauls, already a member of the elite group, Latymer Upper who's governors chose, rightly as it turned out, to become a direct grant school outside the control of the LCC, and St Clement Danes who chose to join the general run of LCC schools. I was lucky to win a place at Latymer and within five years, Latymer was challenging St Pauls, whilst St Clement Danes had sunk into obscurity. That cemented what had been a growing conviction that whilst we might not have been of the "traditional conservative class", theirs was the right way, and however well meaning the Socialist/Labour movement was, their philosophy in practice simply did not work. Certainly the opportunity to go to a great school that my parents could never have afforded, was the one thing the then labour Government under Clement Attlee did not scrap, and it was left to Harold Wilson to shamefully abolish that Direct Grant System that gave me and thousands of working class children, the chance to aim for the sky. That help for working class youngsters was not regained until the Assisted Places Scheme was reintroduced, only to be scrapped again by the second Wilson/Callaghan Government. To me it smacked of a philosophy of "if everyone can't have something, nobody can". That too entrenched my belief in the politics of the centre-right.

My time at Latymer was a reasonably happy one, for though my dyslecsia meant I started in the C stream of a four stream intake, we had exams each year, and by the time I reached the Upper Fifth, I had made the A stream, so perhaps my poor spelling had not set me back too far. That limitation was nearly my undoing, for matriculation at that time demanded five good credits, of which one was a modern language. If my spelling in English left much to be desired, you should have seen my French. However lady luck shone on me, for having on advice, written a letter to an imaginary boy in France, I had it checked for spelling. Low and behold that was one of the options in the exam.

I did not take a particular interest in active politics, perhaps because my classmate was Peter Walker, later to become the MP for Worcester, subsequently a senior cabinet member, and then a life peer, for he seemed to know so much, that I just felt it would be beyond me. We jokingly used to feel that in any debate, Peter would quote chapter and verse, on what someone had said in the House on such and such a date, and that left the rest of us floundering. He and I had the same birthday, but he did not stay for the sixth form declaring that he needed to earn some money so that he could afford to enter Parliament. He wagered ten shillings with me that he would make it in ten years. Eleven years later when he won the by-election for Worcester, I wrote reminding him of the bet, and was duly invited to the Commons for lunch.

When the war ended my school decided to adopt and build a link with a school in Hamburg, and the school captain, David Price, was a brilliant guy who set about raising a collection to first send a group from our school, and then to bring a group from Hamburg to England. At that time, whilst I perhaps felt the same deep anger in regard to the conduct of Germany as most Britons, I had also come face to face with members of my faith who had survived the holocaust, and could not at that time feel any sympathy with the reports that came back of the flattened desolation of Hamburg. I'd seen great flattened areas in London, and was well aware of the tragedy of Coventry and other towns and cities in England, and just could not raise at that time any feelings of forgiveness or reconciliation. A family friend brought a young girl to our home, who they subsequently adopted, and who had survived the concentration camp only through the sacrifice of both her parents. The image of the tattoo on that young girl's arm remains with me to this day. When David came collecting, he quietly said, Martin I understand, you don't need to contribute. That association with my old school still exists, and looking back it was the right thing to do, for we cannot hold forever the sins of the fathers on the subsequent generations.

At that time, I had no idea that the holocaust had touched my family, for certainly on my father's side we had been here for hundreds of years, and on my mother's for around a hundred and fifty. But following my election in 1983, a man wrote to me from Amsterdam, having seen the results on television, asking if I was related to the Dr Brandon-Bravo who had practiced there before the war, survived the Japanese prison camp, and briefly practiced again on his return to Holland. I replied that although I was unaware of that branch of the family, he was almost certainly related, since we had never found anyone with that name where we couldn't find a link. When my brother Michael took early retirement as Vice Provost of the City of London University, he and his wife went to Holland to do some family research. He returned with a printout of that branch of our family who had lived both in Amsterdam and Den Haag. There in the list, jumping out at me was an unknown cousin, born as I was in 1932, but died in Auschwitz 1942. It leaves me cold to this day.

My biggest problem at school was coping with the fact that along with just one other in my year group, I was Jewish, and anti Semitism was alive and well. Some of my faith became hardened and strengthened by such taunts as you f****** Jew, but I have to admit at that time to lacking the confidence to cope. I couldn't understand the jibes, since I knew I'd been British long before some of my accusers, and when told to go back to Palestine only made it harder to understand. Much as by then I understood the desire and need for the survivors of the holocaust to have a land of their own, and was delighted when the United Nations created the State of Israel, the terrible things that had happened in the run up to it's creation, added to the anti Semitism, and that drove me further into my shell. The killing of the two British Soldiers in a reprisal to some offence by the army, and the bombing of the King David Hotel gave ample ammunition to those who, whatever the rights and wrongs in those last days of the Mandate, were only too happy to stoke the age old flames of anti-Semitism. In the first few years at Latymer I'd had a very good friend who suddenly said he couldn't be friends or speak to me any more. His parents hearing I was Jewish banned him from having anything more to do with me. If I hadn't been well below average height and about seven stone nothing, things might have been different and I might have reacted differently to what amounted to a form of bullying. However by the age of fourteen I was boxing at under eight stone, and just about holding my own. Being lousy at ball games, I took to athletics and rowing, and coxed the first boat in my last two years at school.

My Patrol "The Owls" of Chiswick

In those years leading to the end of the war, and to 1950 when I left, rationing made school dinners at times hard to stomach, but we were rightly reproached for any waste. However in the sixth form we were allowed to either go home for lunch, or as many of us preferred, to cross the road from the school where a greasy spoon style café put on great lunches. The atmosphere was fun and the layout was in cubicles with tables for four or six. The waitress would come to the table, ask what we wanted and would then turn and holler to the kitchen at the back – one meat pie and chips, one pie mash and peas, and one without peas. I don't ever remember her getting an order wrong, and the cost was no greater than the school dinner.

I did not fancy the school cadet force, for shortly after coming to west London, my brother had made contact with a Scout Group, and at the age of eight, I with one other youngster, became the first members of the 3rd Chiswick Cub Pack, attached to the Scout and Rover Group. It was an unusual group, being completely open and unattached to any church, which was generally the norm at that time. The Scout Master was known only as Colonel, and his wife Gray, became the cub mistress. They were a great pair, and I and hundreds of others, owe a great deal to them, and that's why I stayed with the Scouts rather than join the cadets at school. The group had an excellent working relationship with a group of female Sea Cadets, and a couple of marriages sealed that relationship.

The Rovers were a great bunch, and when they returned from their war service, some had some great stories to tell. One Ginger Cole, had been in the Far East as a driver, and told of the time when in India he was driving in the dark, and misjudged a roundabout on which a cow was sleeping. He recalled a bump when he hit the roundabout, another just after, and then one as he dropped down the other side. When they heard the following morning that a cow had been killed, he kept his head down and said nothing ! Another, Gerald Kosterlitz had been in the Eighth Army in North Africa, as a tank driver. His tank was hit, and he was the only survivor. His family had been refugees from Nazi Germany in the thirties, and his father had been in the Kaisers Army in the First World War His father said that they could withstand a straightforward bayonet charge from the Brits, didn't mind when the bagpipes brought on the Scots, but the ones they really hated were the little brown men with a rag round one hand, and a kukri in the other. The Ghurkhas he said, would strike fear into anyone! Another, Charlie King, by then too old for active service, was the local butcher in Turnham Green, but any resemblance to Corporal Jones, the butcher from Dad's Army, was a million miles from the guy that was Charlie.

I enjoyed the open air life the Group encouraged, and we camped as often as possible. We had a regular camp site on a farm near Ruislip, and I remember with pain the struggle to cycle with a pack on a small bike, up the Great West Road from where we lived on the borders of Chiswick. On one of our badge challenges, I as patrol Leader, and my number two, Derek Gidney, did a weekend trek, and camped on an old golf course that was available to scouts. The weather was awful, and we pitched a small "Itizer" low lying circular tent, and bedded down for the night. The rain was torrential, and one of the resident scout staff came to see we were OK, for all the rest had either been washed or blown away. We survived a few more hours, but in the end realised we would have to gather as much as we could, and get to the safety of the main building. With all our gear over our heads we made a beeline for the building, and it was just as well there was a great flash of lightening, for we found ourselves standing on the edge of a large bunker. In the dark, who knows what might have been the outcome, but all ended well, and we got our badge!

On one occasion we camped on a high bluff close to Branscombe in Devon. The winding road down through the village lead to a bakery half way down, where the smell of fresh baked bread was just too great to resist. One morning we scrambled down to the beach to meet the early returning fisherman, and I have to say that fresh mackerel cooked over a wood fire, with fresh crusty bread, tasted far better than any haut cuisine can ever achieve.

On an earlier camp when I was perhaps eleven or twelve, we found a site in a field alongside the rail track in Llandogo in Herefordshire. Two things from that camp remain in my memory forever. On the far side of the track was a steep well wooded hill, and a group of us set out to climb to the top, either to see if there was anything there, a house perhaps, but if not to see a wider view of the valley and town. When we reached the top, there was indeed a house, hidden away amongst the bushes and trees, and it had a run down but mysterious air about it. This mystery was heightened when an old lady came out to meet us, and I for one began to get the creeps, and thoughts of Hansel and Gretel ran through a few of our minds. She invited us in, and with much trepidation we followed her to find a home, dark, and to our young minds, quite foreboding, with a wide range of Chinese and other oriental collectables adding to the air of mystery. Frankly when she struck the giant brass gong in the main hall, I wasn't the only one feeling the s****. In truth she welcomed our visit, for I suspect few in the village ever went up to see her, so we did get out alive. On returning to camp, the recounting of our brave climb sounded much braver and more entertaining than the reality had been.

The other incident of that camp, applied to a border collie, and a bad attempt by one of the group to cook a meal from tinned meat and heaven knows what else. The dog always knew when the train was coming, and long before we did. He used to go to the far corner of the field away from the station, and as the train approached, he would race it to the station. On the night of the disastrous meal which no-one could eat, the "cook" scraped it onto a large plate and gave it all to the dog. Whilst he appeared to enjoy eating it, it did not agree with him, any more than it had with the rest of us, for it was two or three days before the dog tried to race the train again.

This incident came to light again over forty years later when a group of colleagues went to Herefordshire to assist in the Monmouth By-election in the eighties. By happy chance I and a couple of other MPs were sent to Llandogo for a spot of canvassing, and we arranged to be picked up later that afternoon at a café overlooking that same field, and where the railway had run all those years ago. Chatting to a local over a cup of tea, I recalled the story of the Border Collie, and to my delight the locals remembered his regular racing of the train, though of course he had long gone to join his doggie mates wherever they go after this life !

In preparation for the World Scout Jamboree in 1947, the Indian contingent stayed with us at our headquarters, for apart from the building, we were lucky enough to own a triangular field formed between two roads, and the path leading to Stamford Brook Underground Station. They were a great crowd, but sadly it coincided with the partition of India, and the creation of Pakistan, for many were unable to return home, either having being told their families had been killed, or they just could not obtain information as to their family's whereabouts. We particularly befriended one Indian who came to our home for supper, and asked us to keep a secret, for he was the only Christian in the contingent. There was a spot of bother over the attempt to arrange a slaughter that would provide acceptable meat for the Muslim scouts, but was the first time many of us, apart from the Rovers like Ginger Cole, had ever had curry, and having a meal with them was something quite new. Apart from the troubles faced by my own people, this was the first time I realised the troubles that existed between the Moslems, the Hindus, the Sikhs and the Christians on the subcontinent. Sadly it is still the same now in the 21st century.

I was at home with the sciences, with practical chemistry as my favourite. I don't recall our chemistry master's proper name, for we only knew him as Dogsbody. I was persuaded at one stage, to produce a stink bomb for friends, and concocted a mixture that produced phenol/iso/cyanide, which cleared the place. Realising that it could be poisonous, and was an extremely stupid thing to have done, I owned up to the Head and was suspended for three days. I could not face my parents with what I'd done, so I duly packed my things as usual on each of those days, and took myself up to the West End of London, to while away the time until returning home at the usual time.

The school rowing club at that time, was run on a proverbial shoestring, for the one fine eight we used, had more shellac and sticky tape holding it together, than it had cedar in it's skin. The school rented racks at the West End Amateur Boat Club, but when that closed we were adopted by the Furnivall Club and stayed with them until many years later the school was able to provide the present splendid boathouse adjacent to the school. Our Captain of Boats was Michael Phelps, the first amateur in his family, for his father was the boatman at Thames Rowing Club. So at the time, we were all made honorary members of Thames Rowing Club, and one of their oldest and most distinguished members, Berry, took pity on us and donated an old but excellent boat, duly named Berry, in which we rowed during my last two years at school.

We did reasonably well in the school league running at that time, but our biggest hate were our neighbours St Pauls. Most schools invited you to tea after a race, but not St Pauls, they just paddled off back to their boathouse, confirming the widely held view of the rest of us, that they just felt superior to all the other schools on the Tideway at that time. The Schools Head one year, had a chaotic start, and when I realised that St Pauls had started, and no one had sent us off, or maybe in the turmoil we hadn't heard the start called, I set us off with a call from the cox's seat. We were furious to find that St Pauls had gone Head, by a couple of seconds, and we were certain, that we would have had that honour had the start not been messed up. To be fair, in 1952 they turned out to be one of the fastest school crews in the country, beating both the London and Thames Rowing Clubs in subsequent regattas. Rowing wasn't the only sport where St Paul's tried to look down on what they considered their inferiors, and showed it again in athletics. Latymer at that time had a great athletics team lead by our geography master Tim Briaux who I believe threw the javelin for GB. The team did win the Schools Championship one year, but when a match with St Pauls was agreed, they would only accept on condition that two or three of our best events were excluded from the match programme.

Because of the examination board we followed, we could not race at Henley Royal Regatta, so Marlow was our prime aim. It was a great regatta, and proudly wearing my shiny new Thames Rowing Club tie, I went to what was known as the long bar, to get a soft drink. I was aware of the rivalry between London and Thames, but without thinking went to the end of the bar, where I found myself surrounded by the giants of the London crew with their navy blue caps with white round the edges. Looking down on me from a great height, one of the crew said "Boy you are at the wrong end of the bar", and I fled for my life to the other end, and into the safe custody of the Thames RC crowd.

Back then, there were two National bodies for our sport, the Amateur Rowing Association, and the National Rowing Association. The former were for amateurs, and the latter, for artisans, i.e. those working with their hands! The School had planned to enter Putney Town Regatta, only to find that it was an NRA event, and we were not allowed to enter. Not until the mid fifties did the two associations merge. That same old Olympian, Berry brought a crew from the London Dock Labour Board to Henley Royal, and our sport became open to all.

I passed what was then the School Certificate, and having matriculated, stayed on into the sixth form. Those two years were the most enjoyable, being treated as adults rather than as kids, but although I passed with good grades the Higher Schools Certificate, the equivalent now of A levels, I failed to win a University Scholarship and opted to do my National Service, and think about the future at a later date.

CHAPTER 3

NATIONAL SERVICE

Having failed to win a scholarship to University; very few made it in 1950, I opted to get my two years National Service out of the way and take stock towards the end of my time. We reported to Oswestry for basic training, and whilst queuing for the required army haircut heard that a half crown pressed into the barbers hand, would leave you at least with some hair. I did this successfully, but it backfired because I volunteered to box for our section, and having done so, fell foul of an observing officer who noted I kept flicking my fringe back. Marched off for a re-cut, it turned out worse than if I'd not bothered to cheat in the first place.

During those first six weeks, we were under a Sergeant Murleader, who whilst of necessity a strict disciplinarian, was quite unlike the characters portrayed in so many films, and took the view that since most of that intake came from reasonable schools, he should not have to repeat himself, and if we played fair with him, he would reciprocate. We did have one disaster, for after carefully ironing our trousers on one of the tables, we found when we finished and removed the blanket, that we had created a felt top to what had been a polished table. I can't remember how many tins of brown polish were used to restore the table to its previous gloss.

In order to be part of the group, I took up smoking and chose Capstan Full Strength just to show my metal, but switched to a pipe before demob two years later. The scene first thing each morning, was a comedy I never missed, for one of the squad had a bed lengthwise along the wall. Half way up the wall was a one inch strip of wooden horizontal beading, on which he would leave a few stub ends of part smoked cigarettes. As he awoke, his hand would creep up the wall, search for the beading, and selecting from the fag-ends, would not open his eyes until he'd had his first puff.

Towards the end of those six weeks, I was granted leave for a day, to attend an interview with a civil service panel with the aim of a possible career in a government science laboratory. I left school with my head full of facts in the world of botany and zoology, but after six weeks of left right, left right, about turn etc, my mind was blank, and I failed most miserably. As it happened it was the best possible outcome, for whilst I might have qualified with a basic degree under a day release scheme, it would never have been at a standard that would have allowed real advancement up the ladder.

My next stop was at Lark Hill camp on the Salisbury Plain, in a gunnery observation regiment. We trained on 25 pounders towed into position by special armoured quads, which on command, stopped, allowed the crew to drop the circular platform under the gun, then went forward drawing the gun onto the platform ready for firing. We were cautioned to keep our feet out of the way when the platform was dropped, and the quad lurched forward, otherwise we would lose a foot, which sadly one of our crowd did.

The regimental Sergeant Major Merryman, was a great guy, and ran a tight ship, and clearly was more in charge than the commissioned officers. Firing practice was fun, but on one occasion when there was a misfire, and the order "cartridge unload" was given, the gun crew froze, failed to unload and started to back away from the gun. The cry went up "get back you bloody national service men".

We acted as "host or base" to regiments and reservists who came for one or two weeks gunnery practice. The pain in the butt were the Royal Horse Artillery, who had such airs and graces that it was hard not to burst out laughing when their conceit came back and bit them in the arse. There was a slope on which they pitched their tents, and then they foolishly parked their mounted guns on the slope above. Needless to say one slipped its brakes and careered down the slope ploughing through their tents.

We all were asked to design a coat of arms for ourselves, and I chose crossed rowing blades and a cox's megaphone, with the motto "Semper in Excreta", but whether it's still on the wall of the hut sixty years on is most unlikely.

Foolishly I did not opt for overseas, and found myself posted to North Wales to an Ack-Ack Regiment near Tymyn (Towyn) then a small seaside town on the Cambrian Coast. Back in 1950 Merioneth was a dry county, and on Sunday the locals promenaded in their Sunday best, and no entertainment was to be seen. A trip into Towyn was hilarious, for the cinema was the Town Hall, and an usherette came round during the interval with a flit spray. Whether this was normal practice, or the recognition that we smelly gunners were in the audience I'm not sure. On leaving the hall, I noticed in a shop window a notice in Welsh and English, a poster stating that all self respecting nations govern themselves, Wales should do likewise, and requested people signed the petition. It was dark, wet, and miserable, and I could not resist wanting to go in and sign! A camp cinema was set up, and I managed to train as a projectionist, and it was certainly much better than the odd trip to the Towyn Town Hall.

Our camp area also operated as a short term training site for other regiments, and on one occasion we had both a Scottish and Geordie regiment on site, and they both ended up in Towyn one Saturday night. There had been a tented bar set up for them, but no-one had bothered to apply for an extension to the licensing hours. That was the first foolish mistake. When the bar closed there was chaos, riot and wreckage, and a call went out to any of our regiment still on site, to muster in order to break riot. Strange how so many of us quickly disappeared into the Welsh countryside. As a result, forward planning required a more careful choice of which regiments were paired with which !

The Gunners
1951

Our Colonel was a boffin who had designed the No 1 Predictor, a piece of kit that first picked up the position of a plane, calculated where it would be by the time the ack-ack shell reached that height, and hopefully therefore would bring it down. In practice, a plane towed a windsock some distance behind it, and the aim was to bring down the windsock. We had a demonstration team, and our colonel had a wager with his opposite number that our team would bring down the windsock on the first day.

Needless to say someone forgot to factor in the length of the tow line, and a high explosive shell burst first time just in front of the nose of the towing plane. It was reported that the pilot radioed down that he was pulling the f****** thing not pushing it.

By February 1952 I was a bombardier at regimental headquarters, and had the sad task of lowering the flag to half mast at the news of the death of King George V1. Later that year, as acting sergeant, for they had tried to get me to sign on, I developed a taste for fillet steak. When the rations were delivered to the regiment, they had to be distributed to the three Messes,- Officers, Sergeants and ORs. So far as the meat was concerned, it was clear that much of the undercut or fillet steak was too good for the Officers, and insufficient for the Sergeants Mess, and would most certainly be lost in a stew for the ORs. Inevitably a decent allocation of these top cuts was set aside for the cooks and the night duty staff. Often the duty Officer would call in late in the evening knowing there was a meal of the best steak available, and I confess that is where I grew to love fillet steak.

Just before my demob was due, my father was seriously ill and I was sent home early and was not required to return for formal demobilisation. My father had a massive heart attack whist in hospital, and after some twelve or more hours with his life in the balance, he pulled through and made a full recovery. At some fifty odd years of age, he lived on to enjoy life until the age of eighty eight. Leaving as I did, I missed the usual goodbye to the camp which the train driver of the push and pull railway operating along the coast always allowed. If there were lads leaving on demob, he'd sound his steam whistle a couple of times, and it was always greeted with cheers all round.

I had made up my mind that either University, or a degree at night school was not possible, and decided to try for a commercial career. Whilst it had clearly improved, my lack of self confidence was never fully overcome until I completed those two years of National Service from 1950 to '52. Before then I was just a kid, but after two years, Taffies, Geordies, Brummies, Scousers, Jocks and all, were real people not just names I'd vaguely heard about, and that was my real growing up. I have no doubt that two years in the ranks was the best thing that could have happened to me, and I can't help but feel that much of our troubles with some young men now, would have been straightened out by a period of National Service.

Strangely that feeling was underscored when I was PPS to John Patten the Minister of State at the Home Office, when the standing committee was dealing with yet another law and justice bill. There had been a lot of comment from both sides with regard to youth problems in the eighties, but as a PPS, the custom was that you sat silently behind your minister. I reached forward and whispered in John's ear, who indicating to the chairman that whilst custom denied my speaking, it should be pointed out that I was the only member of the committee who had served as a National Serviceman, and that the troubles being referred to, escalated once National Service was abandoned. One other very interesting statistic came out of that committee, was that the only time during the 20th Century where violent crime remained static, were the five years following the first and second World Wars. It's a sad commentary on we human beings, that the cathartic effect of the violence of war, dims after five years, and particularly men, revert back to animal instincts.

CHAPTER 4

EARNING A LIVING

Leaving the army, I felt that having watched my older brother spend five evenings and weekends studying at home and at evening classes for an honours degree, whilst working full time at the Department of the Government Chemist, was a commitment I felt I could not face, and decided to try a career in commerce or manufacturing. I admired Michael's dedication and recognised his academic abilities, but for me the prospect of just an ordinary degree that would have lead to an ordinary mundane role buried in some government department had little attraction.

During an interview at Marks and Spencers with a lady called Bessie Werner, I had the chance to either join their trainee managers course, or join one of their suppliers. I was introduced to one of those suppliers, Richard Stump who ran a dress manufacturing business in Nottingham, and I felt I would be more at home in that atmosphere rather than the retail shop floor.

Just as would have been the case at M&S, you started at the bottom, and in my case sorting and logging the vast collection of buttons, that were the stock in trade of a manufacturer of women's clothes. A good friend who chose the M&S store route, was handed a broom as a starting point, and just as the store was about to close, he attempted to stop a little man entering. After a few moments he had to give way, since the little man was none other than Sir Simon Marks, the boss-man on one of his unannounced store visits. My friend did survive to have a successful career with them.

I was found accommodation with a Mrs Annie Caldwell who looked after me like I was family, and because it was close to the factory, I soon found myself opening and closing up, and generally taking on managerial roles. The factory had been the local cinema – The Kinema – with the ground floor now used as working factory space, and what had been the balcony as a cutting room. The projection room had been made into a small but adequate canteen, and visiting suppliers and customers, were impressed at it's conversion following Richard Stump's London factory being destroyed during the Blitz. Local callers always recalled the double seats at the back of the balcony, for those who were less interested in what was being shown.

I attended night school at what was then the Nottingham District Technical College , which became Trent Polytechnic, and latterly now Nottingham Trent University, studying textiles and management techniques. Work study fascinated me, and it was not long before I was given free reign to try to bring sectional priced piece work into our garment manufacturing, which until then had mainly been poorly paid time work, or simple piece work based on a machinist making the whole garment. When breaking down the operations necessary to put a garment together, the easiest operation to measure and price was over-locking, which was a means by which the edges of cut cloth were over-sewn before the parts were put together. We had a Greek girl, known only as Greek Anna, who handled bundles of cloth and her machine in a way, and at a speed, few others could match. Having set those first rates, I found that all the over-lockers had disappeared into the toilets, and having asked one of my supervisors what was going on, I found that the girls were concerned that Greek Anna was earning too much money and that I would therefore be tempted to cut the rates. On assurance that I was happy with the rates set, and that if Anna earned twice as much as the others, well the chance was there for them to watch, learn, and raise their own income. It was pretty plain sailing after that, and steadily all aspects of the manufacturing cycle were covered by sectional piece work rates, raising the income for everyone, including the business.

The textile slump that had kicked in around 1950/2 was a difficult time, for the boom that followed the years of austerity during the war petered out, and I found I had joined the company at a very difficult time in late 1952. The strange thing was that as trade picked up again, the restocking that was necessary, required greater financing, and just as now in 2012, firms were going bust through lack of finance, just when trade was on the up. By the end of 1953 we too ran into difficulty with the local regional manager of Barclays Bank. In short he would not allow an increase in our facility, regardless of the fact that the company had continued to make a profit and was well able service a larger overdraft. We then found that he had taken the same line with many other textile manufacturers in Nottingham all of whom were Jewish run businesses. It was clear that once again anti-semitism was rearing its head. The local branch manager had no power to overrule his regional manger, and directed us to the manager of Martins Bank. The manager was Raymond Usher, who took one look at our accounts and expressed amazement as to why we had been refused facilities, and readily agreed to take our account. In return we recommended, and he accepted, all the other firms that had run foul of Barclays prejudiced way of doing business. It was ironical that some years later, Barclays took over Martins Bank, but by then Barclays had discovered the prejudiced actions of their regional manager, and he had been dismissed.

Adjacent to the factory was a site of equal size occupied by a garage business. The owner was seeking to retire, and it gave us an excellent opportunity to expand the size of the factory. Having bought both his business and the site, we constructed a modern extension of three stories, allowing not simply to the more than doubling of the potential capacity of the business, but it created enough space to bring in some of the modern developments in mechanical handling and production flow. At that time we employed around 200 staff. The business grew steadily, and as demand increased, and as we did more and more business with M&S, another factory was opened in Nottingham's Lace Market, and our staff grew to over 400. Many friends in the trade expressed concern at how big a slice of our capacity went to M&S, but it was sound business, tough, but guaranteed, and in all the years, until I retired from the company in 1983, we had never failed to make a decent profit. I was very much at home as director on the manufacturing side of the business, leaving the selling first to Richard (Rick) Stump the owner and MD, and ultimately to his daughter Wendy, who was a real chip off the old block, was well liked at M&S and who worked with our design team to ensure we were always working at capacity. She could sell the proverbial deepfreeze to Eskimos.

It wasn't all work, for apart from joining the local rowing club, I found myself with a group of men of my age, give or take a year or two, from the Jewish Youth Club, who played cards on a Tuesday evening. We took it in turn to play host, and to provide the food that along with the banter was certainly for me, far more fun than the card game. One Tuesday, in I think the late fifties, the stock market had crashed, and I had been dabbling in small purchases through a local broker. So small were my activities that I dealt with the receptionist rather than one of the partners. I was pretty shattered, for whilst it was only around four or five hundred pounds in shares, it was all I had. Rick Stump assured me that I should not worry, for after all, shares were for the long term and they would recover. The fact that he had also lost a lot was little comfort. We played a game of Auction Solo, and if you bid five tricks or more, you had to cover the kitty in the middle, which on that evening stood at some two pounds ten shillings. I had a good hand, and hesitated to bid and cover the kitty. I'd hesitated so long, that one of the group, Brian Appleby, who later became a Circuit Judge, got on to me, with "the come on, bid or pass, but don't hold the game up" Thinking of how much I'd lost that day, worrying about the tiny kitty on the table seemed ridiculous and I just had hysterics, and eventually explained to the gang the days disaster on the Stock Exchange. However the following morning I rang the receptionist to see what was happening, and she assured me that whatever had triggered the crash that Tuesday, the market had bounced back to where it had been before the crash. Great I said, sell the lot. She said it would take time for they were all small bits and pieces of holdings. She came back at around three that afternoon, and asked what did I know that the brokers didn't ? I asked why, she said, "well you've lost little more than the costs of selling, and after I was clear, the market had crashed again and was lower than it had been at close on the Tuesday". I had to explain that I had just finished reading the Lanny Budd series by Upton Sinclair, where in one of the books, the story of the Wall Street crash of 1929 featured, and the concept of the dead cat bounce became notorious. I got out before the cat came down a second time.

One other card evening that sticks in my mind, was when we were at the home of one of the crowd, Stanley Goldman who ran what we called a "swag" shop. He sold all sorts of small things, toys, trinkets, general domestic stuff, and we used his stock when we ran a fund raising Tombola stall. It was amazing how many small prizes you could get for just ten pounds, to ensure the stall was well provisioned. The room we played in had a large, then fashionable, mirror over the mantelpiece, with another large mirror on another wall.

We had been playing for a while when I realised that Stanley, and indeed others, could if they took the trouble, see the cards of others in the mirrors around the table. We gave him a lot of stick over what he claimed was an innocent error, but we gathered his long playing records and stacked them across the mantelpiece and along the beading or dado rail round the room, to ensure fair play. I can't pinpoint the date, but I do remember that Shirley Bassey was the young rising star at the time, and one of the LPs was hers which included Kiss Me Honey Honey, the song that hit the headlines at that time.

The youth club was a useful link within the Jewish community in Nottingham, and it was frequented by many of the older members, as well as youngsters. On one of my weekends back home in London, my father asked if I'd met any nice people in the community, and I said that of course there were the usual Cohens, Goldbergs etc, but had also met two brothers by the name of Sells. My father thought for a moment and said that I should ask when I met them again, if their real name was either Lopez or Gomez Elzader. If they were Lopez, just shake his hand and say nice to meet you cousin. A few weeks later at a gathering at the club, the brothers were there, the question was put, and they duly owned up to being Sephardic as myself. Now the community in Nottingham were almost entirely rooted in the exodus from Europe in the early 1900s and the thirties, and were Ashkenazi's. There had always been a little tension between themselves and the much earlier settlers, the Sephardim, and the "Sells" had thought best to keep it quiet. There was quite a discussion that followed, but the biggest laugh was when one of the girls, Valerie Bentley, said that now it was all in the open, her family were also Sephardic. The question promptly was asked, what had been their family name. She brought gales of joshing when she admitted that had her father not changed the family name, she would have been Valeresa de Fonseca de Pimentel.

Around 1955 or 56, Rick had given me the chance to buy a small stake in the business, and Raymond Usher readily gave me an overdraft to be able to buy the stock he offered. That small stake was the added incentive to stay and help make the business grow. The business did well and in 1970 we sold a majority stake to a major private company Readsons of Manchester. Rick had had a real cancer scare a couple of years before, and sensibly wanted to secure his family's future, should that scare become a reality. There then followed a reverse takeover by Richard Stump Ltd of a public company Hall and Earl. That gave us extra manufacturing units to take under our wing, a small one in

Cwmbran, one in Newcastle a third in Chester le Street, plus a knitting unit in Leicester and a dyeing and finishing company. The largest manufacturing unit was the Durham Company which I visited on a fortnightly basis, but the staff there were surprised that I took the trouble to walk round the factory greeting everyone. What had been the regular routine in our Nottingham units, simply had never happened under the previous Durham management, yet was just the normal and right thing to do if good industrial relations were to be maintained. It turned out that

Sally in 1968

all such matters previously went through the union, and since their representative was based in Loughborough, it was clear why problems took time to iron out. We'd never had such problems in our Nottingham factories, for on the contrary, our staff who were picketed every few years by the clothing and textile union representatives, always asked that I send them away. I made clear they had the legal right to try to sign the staff up, and we would not stand in their way if they wished to do so, but since we had good working relations with all our staff, no one ever signed up. Every six months, we gathered in the factory canteen, and set out where the company stood, what the prospects were, and so forth, and we found we ran a happy ship.

Rick was a true entrepreneur, and when it was clear that knitted fabrics were coming more and more into fashion, and knowing that yarn and knitting had been part of my textile studies, it was a case of my finding a firm of commission knitters, buying yarn, and producing our own fabrics to offer M & S. To make sure M & S bought into those plans, he bought a small company in London who specialised in knitted dress-wear, and on the basis of their range showed we could supply them with both woven and knitted garments. That purchase took us into the typical West End Fashion World, and by 1964, when I married my wife Sally, she was able to go down to London during the showing time, and model the range for us. It had a double benefit, for the samples having been worn, or rejected for whatever reason, they could not be sold, and she had first choice of whatever she fancied. I'm sure my friends in Nottingham were convinced I'd married an heiress, for she certainly was one of the best dressed around, and bear in mind Nottingham was reputed to have the best looking girls in the country!

We'd met in the most odd of circumstances at a Jazz Night at the Trent Bridge Inn, in the autumn of 1962. M&S had recently persuaded us and a number of their dress manufacturers to handle a very small and uneconomic contract of upmarket garments for a selected number of top stores. It was the brainchild of a daughter of one of the directors, who could not be denied the chance to show what she could do, and we as manufacturers were in no position to refuse. The fabric allocated to us was great in appearance, but an absolute nightmare to handle. It was an American foulard using an artificial Arnell fibre, so woven that it frayed the moment it was cut. We feared that from cutting room to machine floor, the garments would be one or two sizes smaller than planned. Our engineer solved the problem by setting a hot wire into the edging machines, so sealing the edges that we could avoid fraying until the garment had been put together. Because of the length of our cutting tables, we were always left with cloth lengths quite suitable for single dressmaking, and we had regular sales to our staff at a tiny fraction of cost, for whatever it raised, and it raised quite substantial sums, it was better than having to either dump it, or try to sell it to market traders. On this occasion we were only too pleased to sell as much as we could to our staff, even if that meant we only delivered 70% of the contract. The cloth was so distinctive, that when I saw this young slip of a girl sitting with a crowd of hairdressers I knew, all I could say was "Where the hell did you get that cloth". The girls rallied round and told me not to be sharp with her, after all she was relatively new at their

In 1979

salon and she was only 18. She explained that one of my cutters, instead of giving her a tip each week, bought some of our remnants and every month or so gave her a dress length instead of a tip. The girls all worked for the biggest hairdressing salon in Nottingham, with no less than a staff of 50. We reckoned they were the best looking bunch in town, and we lads used to queue up outside the salon to collect our girlfriends at closing time. I apologised, offered to drive her home, and the rest as they say is history.

No computer would have put us together, for she was from a farming family, a real county set, and Church of England. I was a Jewish dress manufacturer from the East End of London, so our backgrounds could not have been more different. Yet we hit it off, and after about a year, I did the proper thing and asked her father if we could get engaged. He wanted the weekend to think about it, for clearly there were problems to consider, but having asked if I would wait a year until she was twenty one, I agreed,

Paul & Joel

and the following week we sealed it by choosing a beautiful sapphire ring. We had to face the fact that we could not marry in a Church or Synagogue, so we had a civil wedding in September 1964 in Oundle near to Fotheringhay where my in-laws farmed. Sally understood that over the centuries, if you were born Jewish, whatever you might or might not believe in after that, you would always be known as a Jew. Even Disraeli who was baptised at the age of eleven, was always known as our first Jewish Prime Minister.

For both of us, our wedding wasn't just the expected happy day, but a great giggle, for the mix of guests gave us much to laugh about long after the event. The mixture of our families, my business friends and some executives from our various businesses, together with the rowing fraternity and the county set, gave us much to chuckle about. Two of our Jewish directors in one of the subsidiaries that manufactured for Mothercare, could never have been on a farm before, and were confronted by father-in-law's enormous Hereford bull. They stopped transfixed by the giant equipment the bull had, and were heard to remark, in a way only Jewish people can say it "You can make a living at this?"

At that time the Tom Jones black bow worn in the hair by many women was all the rage. When my boss Rick and his wife Lily and daughter Wendy arrived, he parked the car, whilst the two women walked to the house. Mother in Law, just assumed that the black bows indicated they were a couple of the waitresses they'd booked and sent them to the back kitchen. They took it in good part, and had a good laugh, though mother-in-law took some time to get over the embarrassment.

We decided to honeymoon in the Holy Land, Israel, and did that both as our preferred choice, and to appease my mother in law, who to be fair had only ever met one other Jewish person before, and was staunchly Church of England. She had a very narrow view of her Christianity, and could never accept that Jesus was a Jew. She insisted he couldn't have been, after all he was a Christian, and no explanation of the history of those times was ever going to change her mind. Over the next couple of years, Sally undertook a period of study to convert to Judaism, for we were determined to be a united family with no religious divisions. We also agreed that if we had children we would bring them up in the Jewish faith, giving them so to speak, a hook to hang their hat on, and what they did when they were adults would be up to them. As it turned out we have two great sons of whom we are justly proud, Paul born in 1967, and Joel in 1971. Both the boys have great families, and we have enormous pleasure and joy in seeing our grandchildren growing up. Our eldest Paul, with an environmental honors degree, after spells in a few jobs and one with RBS, decided he would never work for a corporation again, and is happy running his own gardening business. The youngest made it to Oriel - Oxford - and after a spell in the music industry is now the CEO of the UK branch of Travelzoo, a highly regarded online company in the travel and entertainment business.

I'd never been overly religious, but going to Israel at that time, certainly gave me a feeling I'd not experienced before. The bible became a history book, rather than just a religious tract, and I read it through on return home. At that time, I believe on a Sunday evening, was a TV programme where a very Jewish sounding David Kossoff, a brilliant actor, sat in on large high backed throne, with children gathered at his feet. He read from his version of the Bible, telling the story of those times in his own way, as perhaps only he could. It became reading for our boys whenever I was around at bedtime, which sadly I confess was not as often as I would have wished.

I recall standing in the center of Be'er Sheva by the well in the centre of the old town. The Israelis appeared to have policy of leaving the biblical towns untouched, and building the new alongside the old town, which also carried the old biblical name. Looking down we realised you could not have moved this central well from place to place, and this therefore would have been the same well as had been there since back in biblical times. That sense of history came through in a way I had never experienced, even when visiting old churches or monasteries at home or in Europe. We visited all the well known biblical sites, and down to Elat on the Red Sea. In the desert just north of Elat was a kibbutz, home solely to West German youngsters who felt that helping the desert to grow was in some way helping to put right the evil their elders had committed during WW11. One thing struck us was that on a hill just south of Jerusalem and looking west to the sea, we saw row after row of young trees growing, helping to restore the land from a desert to the land of milk and honey of yesteryear, whilst looking east towards Jordan it was just barren. Sally of course planted the traditional tree that all visitors did, I recall for the equivalent princely sum of seven and sixpence. Many Jewish people from around the world pay to have a grove of trees planted to commemorate someone in their family they may have lost, and an appropriate plaque would be fixed to a tree or rock. However I cannot say that some of the plaques weren't moved around when it was convenient to do so.

Tel Aviv, which was our base, was of course a largely new town, but walking to the adjacent Jaffa took us back centuries. Caesarea, Galilee, the place of the walking on water, the site of the Sermon on the Mount, Nazareth and above all Jerusalem were places where you just soaked up the history of that tiny country. The narrowest part of the country at that time was the site of Latrun, where from the eastern border to the sea was just ten miles. At the southern end of Lake Galilee sits one of the earliest Kibbutz; Degania. At its entrance is a burnt out Syrian tank from the 1948 war, left as a memorial of that conflict, and to show that it was the closest the Syrians got to that settlement. In Jerusalem in the Church of the Holy Sepulchre which was part of the old city and sat on the border, illustrated the problem that still faces everyone today. The "churchyard" to the rear of the church was accessible to us, but at the rear was an archway with a notice forbidding further access since we would then have

Three views of our house in 1966 (top) and in 2011

been in Jordan. We inevitably had to have a photo of Sally standing right on that border. Worse was the sight of the Mandelbaum Gate crossing, with barbed wire across parts of the road, again distinguishing between Israel and Jordan. Whatever the hoped for outcome of any peace agreement, I cannot see anyone wanting or agreeing to see the City of Jerusalem divided in that way again. Of course there has to be proper recognition of the rights of Palestinians and other Islamic people being able to visit unhindered their holy sites, just as Jewish people must also be free to visit the Western Wall. At a later trip to Israel, when I put the point to Shimon Peres, he remarked that a vaticanisation of Temple Mount had always been on the table.

Just in the north of the country we were invited by a young Arab boy to enter his garden and join him for some tea. He had a patio overlooking his field, and there was a donkey walking slowly round and round a central pole, dragging a steel sheet behind it. It was an ancient way of threshing corn. He was happy to be an Arab Israeli, and at that time some 250,000 Arabs had remained within those 1948 boundaries. I have never understood why it is OK for Arabs to be able to live in Israel, and not the other way round, for there is no reason why people of differing faiths cannot live in peace with one another in the same patch of land. People will recall, that when the West came to the aid of Kuwait, the troops had to obtain special dispensation to be able to hold a Christian service, in what are claimed to be the exclusive lands of Islam. These are just some of the stumbling blocks to peace in that part of the world.

We set up home in my flat in the Nottingham Park, situated in the centre of the City, giving ourselves time to decide where we wanted to make our permanent home. I'd lived there for nine years before I met Sally, and it had been a place of refuge and overnight accommodation for many of my rowing colleagues over those years. After only eighteen months, Sally spotted an advert for an old farm house, well within the twelve mile radius from the factory that I felt would be manageable bearing in mind early opening and closing of the factory. It was a timber framed and brick building, roofed with old hand made pantiles, and may have been the "Old Farm" part of the estate including Barton in Fabis which belonged to the Clifton family from the 15th century. In it's earliest appearance it may have been one or more cottages, which over the years were brought together, but certainly it was a single property at the time of the Civil War. Charles 1st came through the village, crossing the river Trent on the ferry which operated until 1965, and raised his standard on what is now called Standard Hill in Nottingham.

It was semi-derelict, and the farmer and his brother had moved to smaller homes in the village a few years earlier, but rejected advice from a local developer to knock it down and sell it as a cleared site. Apart from it being a listed building, he could not see his old family home wiped away, and given that Sally had grown up in such homes, she could see its potential. Two of the upper bedrooms feature Yorkshire sliding panel windows, where the central panel is protected by iron bars making them secure rooms that would have served as such during the Civil War. When the roof was restored in 1966/7 almost perfectly ball shaped rocks were found in the roof, which were likely to have been "weapons" used in the war. One has been kept as a souvenir. It has been said that there was a tunnel from the house to the church 100 yards away, but the passage of time has probably closed it in. A previous owner indicated that as late as the early part of the 20th century, the house still featured a "priest hole", adding further to the belief in the tunnel. The main residential accommodation was on the ground and first floor, but when our eldest got into Heavy Metal, we converted two spare rooms in what from the outside was roof space, but was a level covering six unused rooms where years back the farm hands would have lived. At least with Paul settled at the far end, well away from our end of the house, peace reigned. In the garden is a barn which we converted initially into a hairdressing salon, and subsequently into my Parliamentary office on the ground floor, and an artist studio on the first floor. It is a house and home full of history and interest, and has been a great family home until this day.

Within a year, we had at least got the basics in place – we didn't have a kitchen for six weeks – and over the next ten or twelve years turned it into a great country residence. In those early months we had quite a few friends round to see what we had purchased, and initially most thought we were quite mad to have taken it on. However in no time at all, most were searching the countryside for similar opportunities, and after a year it was clear we had made the right choice and felt settled. I had always paid a subscription to the local City Conservative Association, at least when they bothered to come round and collect it, but then felt I should formally join the Rushcliffe Association of which Barton in Fabis was a part, and take some small part in the local community and party. A Young Conservative called to see if we wanted to join, but Sally as politely as she could said that I was just a bit too old for that, but in no time at all the message had reached a great local character Norman Beeby, who promptly signed me up, and before he'd left I found myself as treasurer of the village association. Any political party with a Norman as a member and fund-raiser, would never be short of either members or money.

The year after our marriage, we took a cruise holiday around the Greek Islands on a small one class boat, the Mikonos. The purser looking at our name assumed we were, or spoke, Spanish, and sat us a small table with a couple by the name of Anatheresa and Theodoro Harmsen. They were Peruvians from Lima, who spoke good English and we struck up a friendship which has lasted until now. We met up with them many times on their trips to England, and in 1999 following the World Rowing Championships in Canada, we flew to Lima for a wonderful three weeks in that fascinating country. With Theo's excellent relationships with the local travel agent, Wagon Lit, a great trip was organised for us, and we visited Arequipa, Cuzco, Machu Picchu, and of course I had to climb the mountain that always features in photographs of that wonderful site, Huayna Picchu. Its not as difficult as it looks for there are aids for climbers, but at 68 years of age I had to sign myself in and out – they don't like to leave visitors up there – and I entered the book with the comment that the old goat made it ! A trip over the Andes was included, and we spent a few days in a "jungle" holiday village. A guide accompanied by a local tribesman explained the medicinal properties of many of the trees and plants, and we were fascinated by what translated as the "telephone" tree. The trunk threw out solid buttresses so that by standing between two of them, you could thump the buttress which would resonate sound for a couple of kilometres and thereby communicate one's position. Theo was the President of a major civil engineering and architect company in Peru, and he turned out to be a world authority on concrete. A few years ago at the age of ninety, he updated his textbook on the subject, to an encyclopaedia of 800 pages. I never thought there could be so much to say about the stuff. When the BP oil rig exploded in the Gulf of Mexico, I rang him to say that if only BP had contacted him, they might have used the right kind of concrete !

Given the size of the house, we could again play host to both rowing and political colleagues, and over the years we've lost count of the great names in both rowing and politics whose company we have enjoyed at Barton. Perhaps one of the most interesting rowing guests was Bob Janousek, who following the sadly aborted break for freedom by Czechslovakia in 1968, managed to be granted leave to become our National coach, and he stayed with us for a couple of weeks whilst he sought a place to live, given that the idea was to establish a squad at Holme Pierrepont, which was completed in 1971, and formally opened in 72. Having also managed to have his family join him, there was clearly no way he was going back, once the "revolution" was quelled, and because of the risks involved, he could not travel with his crews to Eastern European regattas.

We returned to Israel again in 1967 to help in some small way in what turned out to be a Six Day War. However we arrived on the Monday after the cease fire that Sunday afternoon, so they must have heard we were coming ! I'm not sure what drove that reckless decision, but it was Sally who spoke to our bank manager and asked for an overdraft since I was up to my limit. When he knew what it was for, he readily agreed, something I doubt would happen now in 2012. When I arrived home from the factory, Sally simply said, order the plane tickets, we'll find accommodation when we get there. At the airport we met a

Nottingham friend, Monty Alge, whose brother had emigrated to Israel a few years earlier, and was now a fisherman on Lake Galilee. A youngish non-Jewish man was also on our trip, but because he was over forty he was paying his own fare, for he just wanted to help in any way he could. Under forty and you could fly EL AL for free if you wanted to help them in that war. It was interesting that of all the foreign helpers, the greatest number came from West Germany.

On the first night we stayed at a small boarding house which displayed the equivalent of our Blue Plaques indicating that Menachim Begin the leader of Irgun, and subsequently the Prime Minister, had lived there. We hired a car and made our way to Jerusalem and had the chance to approach the Western Wall in the Old City, but had to follow the parallel lines of tape, for they were still setting off unexploded armaments left around on the ground beyond the tapes. As relaxed and less than religiously observant as I was, I still found standing before the Western Wall of the Biblical Temple an unforgettable and emotional experience, and can understand how Israelis will never countenance giving up their rights to Old Jerusalem.

We moved on to kibbutz Nof Genosar on Lake Galilee where our Nottingham friend's brother had settled, and happily agreed to eat with the kibbutznics in their communal hall. Most of the kibbutznics had joined their army units, and as a result they had closed the hotel which they ran to help fund the running of the kibbutz. We crossed Galilee in one of the two fishing boats run by the kibbutz, one an old Thames tug, and the other a Swedish tug. On the far side, our host pointed out that they rarely came this far, otherwise they would risk being shot at by the Syrians from the strongholds of the Golan Heights and from the hillside overlooking the lake. We noted the UN pillbox on the shoreline, and asked what the UN role was. We were told that if there was an incident, the UN soldiers on duty would come out with their clipboards, note the incident and go back in. It was abundantly clear as to why the Israelis were so dismissive of UN resolutions.

We went round to the east side of the lake and found a compound with rows and rows of captured Jordanian tanks. I pulled out my camera and took a snap, only to be arrested by a gorgeous young second lieutenant, who made clear she had to take out my film roll. Her troops promptly took Sally round to show her the tanks, and what struck us as very odd, since we'd heard of the efficiency of the Jordanian Army, was that the equipment in the tanks was still covered in the heavy factory preserving grease, and would have been in no state to have been used in battle.

We revisited the artist's colony Ein Hod in the hills above Haifa, for we had enjoyed the statues and the paintings we'd seen there on our honeymoon, but on this occasion we wanted to know if it had survived untouched by the six day war. The curator of the museum met us, and made clear they had remained unharmed. Her husband was an officer on the Israel/Syrian border, and he'd phoned her during the fighting to see if she was alright, and was reassured that the village had seen nothing of the conflict. Driving back we were hailed down by an Israeli soldier, popping home for a few hours to ensure his family were alright. He looked just like the historical images of Darius, King of the Persians, with his dark skin and chisel beard, and sat in the back with his Uzi across his knees. His English was quite good, and explained that these brief breaks from the front were quite normal now that the situation was well under control. We only stayed for a week, and were not needed for any kind of work, but it was an experience neither of us would have missed.

Wendy Stump who was married at that time to Yuram Polani the son of a long established Jewish/Israeli family, also arrived after the ceasefire , and upstaged us by getting herself down through the desert to the Suez Canal and dipping her feet in the water. Yuram's mother was the ninth generation of her family in Israel, and his father one of the early settlers in around 1911. He set up a citrus export business, and although Yuram was a very bright guy, sadly he took the view that he was rich enough to do absolutely nothing unless it was of temporary interest, and doubtless was the cause of the eventual breakdown of their marriage.

Our trip to Israel on that occasion, and in those tricky circumstances, caused some amusement at my rowing club. I'd been coaching our combined coxless four, and had invited the Chairman of selectors, Christopher Davidge to come to Nottingham and cast his eye over the crew. Realising I'd be away on the evening planned, my good friend and opposite number at Burton Leander Rowing Club, Pym Berry, came over to stand in for me, and he explained my absence to Chris. Davidge paused for a moment, and to laughter all round, he said "Well he always was an impetuous fellow!"

Back home, because part of our group made fleece fabrics, we were also able to move into women's casual sports wear. Rick or Wendy came up with the ideas, and I had to find a way of bringing them into fruition. In the early sixties, we were fortunate to find and employ a terrific designer Jeremy Rangel. He had been born in Spain and had been carried as a baby over the Pyrenees into France to escape the civil war. The family were granted the right to remain, but shortly after he joined our company he realised that he had barely two weeks to get his status sorted out, otherwise he would not have been able to return to France, and as yet had no right to stay in the UK. Happily our solicitor was Victor Mishcon, later to become Lord Mishcon, and this was quickly sorted out. As is often the case with bisexual men, and they are frequently found in the fashion business, he was great fun and above all highly talented. The girls in the buying department at M & S adored him, and he could do no wrong. We could not however restrict him to just designing for the mass production trade that was our bread and butter, and allowed him two days a week to develop his own clientele in bespoke high fashion.

His sexuality expressed itself in a way I had never come across before, in that Eurasian type girls with modest breasts would turn him on, but European women more generously endowed, not only left him cold, but the women knew it and therefore suffered no embarrassment in his presence. He designed the dress with the built in bra, made famous by such stars as Fennella Fielding, Cathy Kirby, Lya Raki from the TV series CRANE, and many others we enjoyed coming through our showroom on Great Portland Street. We developed a new knitted fabric that was coated with vinyl and looked and handled like soft leather. Rick quickly decided we had to do something special with this new cloth, and wanted one of Jeremy's more endowed ladies to model it. Jeremy persuaded Lya to model one of his "bra" dresses for us, and a series of polyphotos were taken to see how we might handle the sale of this new line. It goes without saying it was great fun ogling the collection of photos, and just as I had made some rude noise and expressed the view that they could not be real, Jeremy who had come quietly into the showroom said "Oh Martin they are real, I have seen them". Said in his wonderful franglo accent, left us all falling about with laughter. Inevitably we lost him to the film industry, where he made a real name for himself, designing all the costumes for Maggie Smith in Travels With My Aunt.

Rick Stump and I had got on well with the founder and chairman of Readsons, Stephen Dodson, who had taken up the post war Labour Government's scheme to close down his spinning mills and put the capital raised into something else. Knowing the textile trade, he proceeded to buy up, or buy into, as he did with us, a number of textile manufacturing businesses, covering children's, women's, and gent's garment makers, knitters, dyers and finishers. In short he built a sound integrated group, but did not insist we traded within the group unless it was on a commercially sound basis. The opposite approach was followed by the then Cautaulds Group, who were locked in an incestuous relationship with their subsidiaries, and of course when trade turned down, their whole show collapsed like a pack of cards. Some years earlier Stephen had made his younger brother MD of one of the subsidiaries, and it simply hadn't worked, and Stephen simply took him back as a main board director without any direct responsibility. Sadly when Stephen died, his younger brother Ernest took over the chairmanship, but just as with the subsidiary that failed, he was frankly never up to the task, and he bitterly resented the fact that most of the subsidiaries were successfully run by Jewish part owners or managers We were both on the main board, but when Rick Stump retired, the new chairman made his dislike very clear, so it was not long before I was off the board, and clearly regardless of results, on the way out.

With Sally in 1997

This became very clear, when Ernest decided to take what had become a closed but still quoted company, back into private ownership, and buy up all the minority holdings. As the only member on the board of the public company Hall and Earl, but not on the board of the private Readson company which owned the majority of shares, I found myself negotiating on behalf of all the remaining small shareholders. This level of finance was not my field, but with advice from Lord Victor Mischon, an old friend of Rick's, and a London broking house, a deal was struck, and I obtained a share valuation that Ernest in the end had to accept, and gave me and many employees a nest-egg that allowed me to pursue a new career.

By that time I'd been with the company nearly thirty years, and as much as I enjoyed running the manufacturing side of the business, it was slowly becoming less than challenging, and my interest in active politics was growing. I'd had two spells on the local council, which had its benefits in handling local problems for some of our staff, and by the time I was approaching fifty, I felt I could contribute on the more national scene. I had joined an East Midlands political supper club – The Millbank Club – run by a Leicester man, Maurice Chandler. It was said, granted jokingly, that if Maurice didn't know a particular person, they weren't worth knowing. Our guest on an occasion in 1971 was intended to be my old school friend Peter Walker, but there was presumably a three line whip, and he had to send up a prospective conservative candidate from Central Office, to stand in for him. Put bluntly he was awful, and on the drive back to Nottingham, I remarked to my council colleague, Martin Suthers, that any of our members could have done better; indeed this political novice could have done better. Martin Suthers, who had been a past candidate himself, said well why don't you have a go. It was as simple as that, and the rest as they say, is history.

I was selected to fight the Nottingham East constituency, a typical inner city pocket borough of only a 48,000 electorate. It was a seat by which only a miracle would have taken it from Labour, but Ernest used the opportunity and gave me twelve months notice. The sitting member was Jack Dunnett, who was also the Chairman of Notts County Football Club, so I had an almost impossible task on my hands. The election had not been called by the time the twelve months were up, but the managing director of the parent group, Tom Weatherby, doubtless against the wishes of the chairman, told me to sit tight until the outcome of the election, whenever it came, for it was the time when Jim Callahan failed to call it in October '78. Strangely enough Jack was an orthodox Jew, and I being a Liberal and Progressive, were unusual opponents. At that time the British National Party were trying to get seats in Nottingham and Leicester, and planned marches in the City. The Anti Fascist League, with the best of motives sent us both boxes of literature intended for use against the BNP. Jack phoned me to ask if I was going to use the literature, and when I said I felt it would be counter productive and I had already met with minority groups with advice as to how to handle the situation, Jack agreed. The literature was dumped; the minority groups kept their heads down; stayed away from the BNP meetings which happily turned out to be damp squibs, and all three Nottingham seats failed to raise 1000 votes between them. I managed to raise my share from 32.8% to 39.9% but there are no prizes for coming second and so I failed, as expected, to be elected in the election of 1979.

I assumed that I would be leaving the company, but on being called to Tom Weatherby's office he made clear that if I left under these circumstances, he knew that Wendy Stump would leave too, and that we would set up a new business together supplying M&S and the group would lose a big slice of their business. He persuaded the chairman to let us stay and we created a new group subsidiary Richard Stump (1979) to supply M&S. We did so on the understanding that if I was selected again to fight a general election, I would not be faced with notice to quit, and on my part every effort would be made to ensure that if likely to be selected, or elected, I would do everything to ensure a smooth handover to a new MD.

To the M&S supplying factory in Nottingham was added the responsibility of a factory in South Wales. That business had been owned by yet another of the faith, who employed a first class factory manager, Conrad Meyer, who had been a German prisoner of war, but who had stayed on and married a Welsh lass. The joke at M&S had always been as to whether the owner-Manning - I don't know what his original name was, had ever told Conrad that the war was over ! I used to visit once a fortnight to agree programmes and settle production problems. On one occasion a head poked round the door, and Conrad said "yes Fritz?" It turned out he was the factory mechanic, and yet one more who had stayed behind and made a life here in Wales. Whilst saying my goodbyes, another figure was going round checking doors and windows, when Conrad called out "Heinz", I said, oh surely not another ! I realised then why the factory was so efficient and on the ball. Manning had known what he was doing when he took them on, swallowing whatever reservations he must have had, knowing his background as a refugee from Germany in the thirties.

So it turned out by the time I left the group to enter Parliament following the election in 1983, that nest egg from my share stake allowed me to take a drop of 50% in income, and just about get by with two boys in private day school and a mortgage still to pay. Following the failed 1979 election, the boundaries were adjusted, for the old Nottingham East had, as indicated, been a tiny Labour fiefdom, and the changes made the three Nottingham seats broadly equal. By 1983 the tide which had earlier already begun to turn in Margaret Thatcher's favour, was boosted by the outcome of the Falklands War, and turned what might have been a small chance of success for me, into a clean sweep of all three City seats, for Michael Knowles in East, Richard Ottaway in North, and myself in what had been renamed South. That seat, the old West Nottingham, not the South that had been won by Norman Fowler in 1970, had only once before in living memory, been won by a Conservative back in1959 when the now Sir Peter Tapsell won it narrowly over a senior trade unionist by a couple of hundred votes. It was said that this unlikely result was down to the fact that Peter was a good looking piece of male cheesecake, and all the women fell for him claiming that the narrow victory was down to them. Certainly the Nottingham hairdressers did well out of that election.

I stayed on as a consultant to the group for a couple of years, in order to ensure the smoothest transition, but the new MD appointed by the main board chairman, only underlined the chairman's lack of business acumen and knowhow, for the new MD only made losses. It was sad, for in all the thirty years I had been with Rick Stump, and subsequently working with his daughter Wendy who was sales director, we had never failed to make a decent profit.

After I left Parliament in 1992 I did not want to return to work in the manufacturing textile industry, for there was in any case not a lot left in the mass production side of the industry. However I was offered a part time role by some good friends Maurice and Lesley Sananas in their business which included the GB sales side of the French company NAF NAF. My role was as an expert witness in cases of the counterfeiting of their products, and though not a lawyer, thoroughly enjoyed my time giving evidence, explaining how and why the goods that had been seized were counterfeit. Their family had lived for many years in Egypt and ran a successful textile business there. Following the 1956 Suez crisis, they found their business confiscated, and they had to leave Egypt along with a forced exodus of the large Jewish community who had lived there for many generations, and counted themselves as Jewish Egyptians. A few families stayed on, but as restrictions and pressures grew, they too had to leave, often with little but the clothes on their backs, and dependent on Jewish charities to help them find a country that would offer them sanctuary. It is those expulsions from Egypt and other countries in the Middle East, that underline the refusal by the current Israeli Government, to refuse to accept the right of Palestinians to return to their old homes in what is now Israel.

Being part time, it allowed me to return to Local Government, but also to accept the appointment as President of the Amateur Rowing Association, now re-branded as British Rowing. Fortuitously it also allowed Sally and me to buy a tiny cottage in Henley which turned out to be a boon for all our family. That purchase is a tale in itself, for as long as I can remember, I, and then Sally, always expressed wonderment at the crazy prices of property in that delightful town. As President I found myself driving to Henley for meetings in addition to the regattas we had always enjoyed attending. Staying overnight at either Leander Club or in a hotel was not cheap, so when we went out for a curry on the Friday evening prior to the Women's Henley Regatta in 1996 we could not believe how cheap this delightful, but very old cottage was. I felt sure there had to be something very wrong with it, but having worked out on the back of Sally's cigarette packet – she doesn't smoke any more – that in six months I would qualify for some pension bonus and could, with a bit of help from my friendly bank manager, fund its purchase, I agreed that Sally would enquire as to what was wrong with it. She came to the regatta at lunchtime and said we had an appointment at five, and the deal was done. The flaw was the old roof on this 16th century cottage was sagging and since we had re-roofed our old farmhouse in Barton, this did not put us off. Our friendly builder in Nottingham went down with his mate one Monday morning, finished up on the Friday, with the listed buildings inspector quite happy with what we had done. It has given the whole family a lot of pleasure ever since.

Having dumped my pension pot into the purchase of the cottage, I was taken aback when the following year, Sally was having a quiet drink with one of our neighbours whilst I struggled to get a new refrigerator up a ladder, through the bedroom window, and finally into the kitchen. On joining them, Sally said that our friend Daphne was selling her boat, a Shetland four plus two. Sally saw the negative look on my face, for whilst we had always fancied a gin palace on the Thames, I was nervous at the outlay and running costs – and with justification ! However as Sally put it, "How old was your brother Michael when he died, and how old will you be next year. 66, well buy the b***** boat". She was right of course, and we had great fun for four years with the Shetland, when we swapped it for a bigger craft with an inboard engine, and of course a larger galley for

Sally! Only in 2010 when we were both seriously ill, did we accept that it was too great a risk to keep it and sold it to our friends in the next door cottage in September 2011.

CHAPTER 5

ROWING DAYS

Having as I've said faced up to my lack of hand, foot and eye co-ordination, and taken to rowing and athletics at school, the former became my relaxation, if that's the right word, from business for thirty years, and politics spanning those years and all subsequent time thereafter.

On leaving school and moving to Nottingham as a trainee manager, I found my greatest need for diversion was satisfied when getting down to Trent Bridge and finding there were three clubs there. The first was the Nottingham and Union Rowing Club, and because I was wearing my Thames Rowing Club tie – shameless advertising – I was collared by the then chief coach Freddie Brooks and the skipper Bobby Swift and agreed to join. The other two clubs were the Nottingham Boat Club and the Nottingham Britannia Rowing Club. The "Boat" had been formed in the late eighteen hundreds because the Rowing Club at that time would not permit rowing on a Sunday. The "Brit" was formed to provide artisans the chance to take up our sport, since - as artisans - they could not join either the "Boat" or the Rowing Club, those clubs being affiliated to the Amateur Rowing Association. There was friendly competition between the clubs and the University, and I knew I'd joined the right set-up when at the February Head of the Trent long distance time trial in 1953, my club won the Headship, only to be disqualified on a technical objection from the president of the "Brit".

By then I had put on enough weight, I weighed in at about ten and a half stone, to row rather than Cox, and won a place in the club junior eight planning to race at Chester Regatta. The then classification of junior was not related to age, but what you had won at open regattas. The first stage was Novice, the next Junior, followed by Junior Senior, then Senior and subsequently Elite. Back then there were still crews who rowed on "fixed pins" though most had taken up the modern swivel rowlocks and blades. These fixed pin rowlocks were usually a rectangle formed by a metal base, with two upright metal pins, and a twisted rope across the top to close the rectangle. The blades had a curved leather collar that you drew though the rowlock from the outside, and the curve of the leather collar or button, aided the finish of the stroke. We had no means at that time to take our own racing eight to regattas, and we arranged to borrow a boat from the Royal Chester Rowing Club. We made clear we would bring our own oars for the modern swivel rowlocks, but when we arrived the Chester boatman was, he said on instruction, removing the swivel rowlocks on the boat we were borrowing, and fixing the rectangular rowlocks that could only be used with the old fashioned blades that I and some others had never handled before. Regardless of our protestations, they dismissed us on the basis that since we would certainly lose the first round to the local school, it wasn't worth leaving the boat with swivel rowlocks in place. Nothing could have wound us up more, and after a couple of outings to try out these old blades which they then provided, we duly thumped the school, went on to win the final, and the faces of the officials at prize-giving simply made our day. We had a bit of a comedian in our crew, Colin McKay, who examining the trophies and winners tankards that morning, remarked to the official setting out the pots that the Junior Eights pots were not engraved – the more senior ones did show the title of the event. With a bit of a sneer, the official said "Well we don't know you've won it yet" When it came to the prize-giving and Colin received his tankard from the same official, everyone heard him say "I told you they should have been engraved this morning".

Later that year, I wanted to enter the novice sculls at the Bedford Regatta held then in the week after the Royal Regatta at Henley on Thames. It was one of the biggest non-metropolitan regattas in the country, and with the local club and schools, competition was always fierce. Bobby Swift did not think I was up to the right standard and was not prepared to enter me. I offered to pay my own entry fee, which was seven and sixpence old money, and when it turned out that I would have to race five times to win, he offered to return one and sixpence for each heat should I win any. He thought he was safe, but somehow I had other ideas, perhaps it was my ethnic background, but I raced like hell and won the event. Sitting exhausted just after the finish of the final against a local guy Chris Baron, all I could shout across to the celebrating club members, was "Tell Bobby I want my seven and sixpence back". I don't mind blowing my own trumpet but I'd busted the course record in each successive heat.

I bought a second hand single scull later in the year, and because of business commitments concentrated on sculling rather than seeking a slot in a crew. Because of my size, I was never going to reach above club level but I did get chances to slot into crews, and over the years won my spurs in sweep oar, and sculling, up to elite level. Slotting into crews became a bit of a habit, for on two occasions we had injuries to members of our Henley Eight, and I dropped in as the only substitute allowed back then.

But of course at under 11 stone, if I came across a Steve Redgrave type, I got my arse kicked in no uncertain manner. Sadly there wasn't a lightweight classification back then, but even so I would have had a hard time, for we had a brilliant crop of scullers around that time, and whilst I managed to win at Reading, it was my only success on the Thames.

Our club president Gus Darby, was a wonderful old boy, who looked and lived like someone from the Victorian era. He had a river day boat, The White Lady, that would have graced the Royal Regatta, and stepping into his home in the Park estate in

The Head of the Thames – I'm at No.3

the centre of the City was like stepping back into what at club dinners he always described as that glorious Victorian era. I'd joined the club committee, I suppose representing the younger members, and when it was suggested that the club invested in a gas water heater for the showers, he threw up his hands in horror at such a modern unnecessary extravagance.

In 1957 at the age of 25, I was elected Club Captain, something I could never have dreamed of, but in truth there were senior members of the club with their own agenda, and unbeknown to me, I was chosen as a temporary candidate until they could chose someone of their vintage and standing. Other senior members did not like what they saw happening, and a row broke out between these two senior groups, and I wasn't sufficiently experienced to find a way of nipping it in the bud before it got out of hand. Sadly it did, and five or six of these top guys resigned, including two top athletes Nick Clay and Peter Acred, who were an outstanding pair, and the former perhaps the most outstanding and upcoming single sculler in the country who was quite capable of going all the way to the top.

The guy who effectively drove out these members was a past captain Freddy Brooks, and I admit I did not and could not stand up to him at that time. Happily he was posted abroad to Germany and with his presence removed I set about rebuilding the club. There still remained a good spirit in the club, and we steadily rebuilt our numbers, and rebuilding our reputation in the world of provincial club rowing, putting a decent crew into the Royal Regatta in four of my five years in office. The real breakthrough came when two guys from Leicester who rowed as a pair on the canal that ran through that city, wanted to come to Nottingham for the clear opportunities we could provide. One, Peter Bickley stroked the club eight, and his pair partner Richard Waite, eventually won the Wyfold Cup at the Royal in 1963, going on to represent Great Britain at the world Championships that year, and again on other occasions in a pair with Mike Sweeney who stroked Cambridge three times, and who is now the Chairman of Stewards at the Royal. These two were just the catalyst the club needed, and they helped set the example to the rest of the club as to what could be achieved, even by a comparatively small club. Peter stroked the eight at Reading and when the crew beat the much vaunted Eton Eight, we knew we had arrived.

Richard's career with us was even more outstanding, being part of that 1960 eight, then stroking the club Wyfold Four at Henley for three years, winning in 1963. He raced for the goblets for three years in 64/66, firstly with our Carl Unwin, and twice with Nick Nicholson, who had paired with Marshall from the Britannia club at the Rome Olympics. I arranged for the local boat builder to build a pair for them, for the princely sum of £215, and named it the Sally Anne after my long suffering, but very understanding wife. We sold it some twenty five years later to Newark Rowing club as a training boat for £200. A boat like that today could cost anything between four and six thousand pounds dependant on the standard of competition it was planned for, illustrating how times and costs have changed. In the late summer of 1962, I was lucky enough to drop into a four stroked by Richard (Dicky) winning the West of England Cup against our friendly rivals from Derby in the final, and again on the Monday at Ross on Wye.

We set up a combined club arrangement in the region in order to give any outstanding oarsman the chance to race at the highest level, creating on the advice of Graham Ricketts, then Chairman of Stewards, firstly a new registered club under the title of Nottingham City Rowing Club, and subsequently Midland Nautilus. Under that latter title they raced for the top Stewards Trophy at the Royal in 1967, winning it in 1968. I believe they should have won the event in 67, but for the outrageous action of the umpire, John Garton, who allowed the Dutch crew to crowd our four against the booms without issuing any warning, and having as a result lost almost a length, finally lost by half a length. As carefully as I could control my anger at such unfairness, I asked why no action had been taken, to be told by Garton that he decided not to act since he felt the Dutch were the better crew. I replied that I did not think that was the role of the umpire, and so began my years of conflict with him. Our crew should have gone to the Mexico Olympics in 1968, but that is explained later

Richard represented GB in 1966 in Bled in what is now Slovenia, and again in Vichy at the Championships in France. Teaming up with Mike Sweeney, these two, by modern standards comparatively modest sized people were still good enough to represent GB in the Canadian World Championships in 1970. Sally and I drove to Bled for those Championships, staying in

Karlsruhe on our first night. It was the first time since the end of the Second World War that I could bring myself to set foot in Germany. As foolish as it may seem, prior to that visit it was just something that emotionally I could not face. I had a lousy night's sleep, only to discover the following day that we had picked the hotel that had been the Gestapo headquarters during the Nazi era. Crossing into Austria we stayed a night, costing ten shillings old money for bed and breakfast in a small village Anif in the shadow of the Unterberg mountain. On into Yugoslavia, and what is now Slovinia, Bled is a magic place set in beautiful countryside, and again for the same cost as in Anif, we were allocated bed and breakfast at the home of a Frau Branco. What always sticks in my mind is that the agency allocating accommodation was called the "compost", and that umpires in Serbo-Croatian are known as "sodniks". I can't think of a more appropriate title !

One Whitsun weekend in 1960, our senior eight had entered the Regatta at Chester on the Saturday, and Hereford on the following Whit Monday. Our number two man, could not make the Chester race and as coach I dropped in as had been my lot on many occasions over the years. We were delighted to beat Royal Chester in round one, and Portora in the semi-final. Racing Shrewsbury School in the final, we won by half a length in a tough race, for schoolboys just never know when they're beat! The Captain of their crew came round to offer his congratulations, and sought to shake my hand whilst I was sitting exhausted in the boat. "Congratulations sir, but we'll reverse that on Monday in Hereford". I replied "Many thanks, but I'm sorry lad you've missed your chance, for I'm only the coach substituting for the real guy who'll be in the boat on Monday!"

The one occasion we did not enter a crew at the Royal, resulted from our lack of technical skills to properly evaluate the quality of a crew. Our greatest opposition in the late fifties and sixties were our friends in the Burton Leander Rowing Club, and our only measure of our standard was whether we could beat the

With my Double Sculls partner Mike Collier

Burton crew. They narrowly beat our four in the provincial regattas, and the decision was therefore made that we would not let our crew go forward to the Royal. Pity we did not know just how good both crews were, for the Burton Leander crew went on to win the Wyfold Cup at the 1959 Royal Regatta.

To illustrate, not just our lack of technical information and skills, but the same applied to the selection of British crews for World and Olympic Championships. Standard qualifying times were set for each event, but the trouble was that we did not have any still water on which to set trials. On the Henley reach, one of the coaches to the GB team was Geoffrey Page, and he used to float a stick – like Winnie the Poo – past the Leander stage, and having timed it, calculated the strength of the stream, and hence was able to correct the standard time required for a crew to qualify. Such rule of thumb would bring gales of derision from modern coaches, but that's the way it was. Of course all that changed once Holme Pierrepont was built, and GB has never looked back since.

Back in the fifties very few women rowed, and certainly none did so in the provinces. One Sunday morning I was stuck for a cox for one of the crews and we put a thick sweater onto the young sister of one of the crew members. With a woolly hat to round it off, I felt we could get away with it, but when Gus Darby made his customary visit to the club, he pointed with a shaking finger at the crew exclaiming "Mr Captain, there's a woman in that boat"! I apologised and promised it would not happen again, and it was years before my club finally allowed women to join.

I suppose my active interest in politics began back to 1966/7, for having completed five years as Club Captain, I took on five years as club secretary, and planning and organisation took up more and more of my leisure time away from the business. At that time, the provincial clubs were looked down upon by the metropolitan clubs, and the officers of the governing body, used to come to a meeting in Birmingham of all provincial clubs, and there we were informed of how they intended our sport was to be run. As mere provincials, after all what did we know about the finer arts of rowing ! That frankly got up our noses, and when elected to the City Council in 1968, I had a taste of what could be done, and how to go about it. That year was also the time when a real gentleman Freddy Page, the father of Geoffrey, was the senior officer at the ARA and he led the reorganisation of the association, arranging for elections for all the provincial regions. My colleagues in the Derby, Burton and Newark clubs, put me forward and I was elected to represent the East Midlands Region.

I made my first mistake, in that I believed I was elected to represent the East Midlands on the National Council, and not the National Council in the East Midlands. Sadly some of the establishment still clung to the notion that we were there to listen and not be heard. Thus was my training in the politics to come. That year too, was Olympic year with the games in Mexico City. By then we had put together a joint crew from our club and Derby Rowing club, which was unbeaten in England, winning the Stewards Cup at Henley, and was undoubtedly the best in the country in that class of boat. The selection board had decided that qualification would be based solely on the outcome of the regatta in Amsterdam. The course which has since been reconstructed, had a problem with the wind, which, if it was a following wind, would spin off the grandstand at the finish, and after a few days would have the water on the course slowly circulating making it grossly unfair. The Dutch made clear that they would not use the results for their own selection purposes, but for some obscure reason, one member of our selection panel insisted that any result should stand, regardless of how unfair the results turned out. It was calculated that a sculler in lane six, the most affected lane, would be 17 seconds slower than his equal in lane one ! That member, Colin Porter, who had been one of our successful internationals and supposedly the athlete's friend, seemed able to overrule the Chairman Christopher Davidge who was the only Gold medallist we'd had in many years, and the rest of the selection panel likewise seemed unable to challenge Colin's dogmatic view.

There followed three special meetings of the National Council, but because there was no mechanism for overturning the selection committee's decisions, and with everyone knowing how outrageously unfair the process had been, we all felt deeply frustrated and angry for the athletes who were being denied the once in a lifetime chance of representing GB in the Olympic Games. I do not recall any member of the National Council, speaking up for the selectors view, and all were angry at their intransigence. It was the worst possible example of an establishment group, imposing it's will on what was at the time the first properly and democratically elected National Council.

Our four which had been unbeaten until the regatta in Amsterdam, had finished third in an affected lane, beating the Italians who went on to win the Bronze medal in Mexico. Our President at that time was Harold Ricketts, and I felt he was genuinely sympathetic to our case. He however took me to one side and pointed out what damage I might be doing to the Association. Whilst thanking him for his genuine courtesy I had to reply that perhaps the Association should consider what damage they were doing to the athletes involved. I had written to Denis Howell, then Minster of Sport, and Harold and Freddie Page went to see him. Given his view that the resolution of selection was a matter for the Association, he did give his consent for its review. The Minister agreed that the National Council at a third meeting, should have a chance to review the selection. Harold therefore allowed the calling of that third Council meeting, and with the Minister's nod in our direction favourable, I had great hopes the logjam would be broken, but all to no avail. Porter would not budge, and our crew, and a coxed four from the Poplar and Blackwell Club were told at that third Council meeting that nothing could be done.

What made it worse, was that Porter had written to the Council making what many would see as a racist reference to my background, and therefore what did I know compared to him. Jack Beresford our five times pre and post war Olympic Champion contacted me and felt I had every reason to sue on the basis of the letter, but I thanked him for his concern and support, but felt I would not climb into the same gutter as Colin Porter. Whatever odium I might have suffered, it was nothing compared to the disappointment for the crew that had sweated for months to achieve their Olympic goal, only to have it snatched away by a selector who had been chosen as a champion of the athletes. All that was achieved by this debacle was that the system was changed, and selection has since been vastly improved, but nothing can take away the bitter taste that must remain with the members of the two crews who were denied a lifetime ambition to represent their country at an Olympic Games.

Asking awkward questions, and "not knowing my place" had it's downside, for I discovered some years later that somebody on two occasions had nominated me for membership of Leander under the over 40 years of age and services to Rowing criteria, but had been requested to withdraw the nomination to avoid a Black Ball situation. Unaware of this, and never likely to meet the outstanding rowing performance criteria, much as I would have been honoured to have been elected, it simply didn't concern me, I discovered this sometime in the early seventies when taken to one side by Graham Ricketts, Harold's brother, whilst in the Steward's Enclosure at the Regatta. He was most concerned for me, since it was clear that someone had suggested my nomination again and whilst acknowledging my contribution to the sport, he did not wish to see me publicly embarrassed. Sally was with me at the time, and was furious, and said that we had never sought to be where we were not welcome, but that would certainly not deter me from the work I did for Rowing. A few years later, I had a most generous and welcome letter jointly signed by Desmond Hill and Richard Burnell, who had discovered, what they described as this grave injustice, and whilst they would understand if I rejected their offer, they would be pleased to be my sponsors for a fresh application. Coming from two of the most distinguished members of Leander, I was delighted to accept.

Like most amateur sports, raising money was a necessity, for subscriptions would never cover the cost of boats and equipment, and quite fortuitously when Sally and I became engaged in 1963 we had a party at the clubhouse, with a group, the name of which I've long forgotten. But what it did was to highlight the possibilities of running gigs at the club, and raise money that way. Our neighbours at the "Boat" did the same, and at one stage on a Friday or Saturday night, when all three clubs had gigs, I'm certain there were more people down on Trentside, than had ever attended the Cavern – Beatles or no Beatles. The honours board that still hangs on the wall in the clubroom, testifies to the famous groups that played at the Union throughout the sixties.

One Saturday night when all three clubs had gigs on the go, and the clubs were crowded with revellers, three thugs decided to come down to the river and disrupt and cause trouble at one of the clubs. Why they passed by both the Union and the Boat, and choosing to tackle the Brit will be something they doubtless just about survived to regret. Three or four of the Britannia members enjoyed professional wrestling as a sideline, and proceeded to take the thugs apart. Kevin Bruton, who was running our club event at the time, became concerned for their lives and phoned the police. Having explained what was happening, and assuring the police that the clubs were fine and it was the thugs that were taking the hammering, and were ending up in the river, they said that all seemed well and that they would therefore just call down in about thirty minutes time. The word must have got around for neither of the clubs had any trouble thereafter. Would that modern policing would allow such sensible reaction to people defending their property and functions.

I travelled with our club crew to the World Championships in Denmark in the autumn of 1963, and the sight of six lane racing whetted my appetite, not only to find a site in England, but to study and obtain an International Umpires Licence. The crew of Richard Waite, Carl Unwin, Mike Gillott, and John Garton had won the Wyfold event at the Royal for the first time in the club's history, and this was the first major Championships in which our club had ever featured since we had represented the UK in the 1928 Olympics in Amsterdam. Sadly that lack of experience showed in a performance we knew was well below what they could and should have achieved. My former aim was achieved in 1971 and being the first of it's kind in the UK it forms a small chapter later in the book. The latter was achieved in 1970, and I held that licence until I retired under International rules when I reached 65. That year I believe was when Egypt and Syria briefly formed the United Arab Republic, and they brought an eight to the championships held on a lake just outside Copenhagen. Their coach was a big guy called Fayaz Yakan, with whom I eventually became quite friendly. The laugh was that as his crew came into the landing stages, the whole British contingent was standing some thirty yards away watching them disembarque. Fayaz scanned the crowd and made a beeline straight for me, requesting that he wished to meet the British Chief coach or Chef de Commission. I politely steered him to

Jack Beresford, and when he was out of hearing, our group chuckled that out of some thirty Brits, the one guy the Arab picked out, was the only Jew in the team. Fayaz heard about this later, saw the funny side and came to shake my hand and establish a friendship which lasted for many years until his death. Fayaz had been a brigadier in Nasser's army, and he regretted that he'd never made it to the Golan Heights. However we met up when Sally and I visited Egypt some years later, by which time he had become a travel guide, and explained that now there was peace between Israel and Egypt, he'd finally made it to the Golan Heights.

Holding that FISA licence, allowed me to join the Association's International Umpires Committee, which had the responsibility of training and approving candidates for the new National Multilane Umpires Qualification, and to recommend one or two each year for training and recommendation to the International (FISA) commission for the granting of licences to allow those qualified to apply for and hopefully be granted duties at International Championships. Since those days, training and experience has moved on, and you frequently find FISA

A charity row with thelads

candidate and qualified umpires travelling to national regattas all over Europe, both to gain regular practical experience, and to ensure an ever higher standard of regatta management.

One example of how practice brought about change, was our experience at the 1986 Commonwealth Games Regatta at Strathclyde. Prior to this event, the official starting and race control was conducted in French, with Attention - Et Vous Pret - followed by Parte. It was never satisfactory, for multi-syllable words inevitably caused false starts. To add to that problem was the rule that the starter could not start the race if just one hand was raised in any of the crews, which in an eights event was a chance of 54 to 1 on, that someone would indicate they were not ready. We agreed that at the Commonwealth event we would stick to English with, Attention – Set – Go. That was simple and should have been sufficient, but in the final for the Blue Ribbon event for the eights, I had charge of the start assisted by Mike Walker. The wind had got up, and being across, the crews were having great difficulty attaching to the start pontoons. After considerable delay the New Zealand crew, understandably getting cold and wound up, set off on a false start even before any orders were given. When they reattached, I did as politely as I could, suggest that they might wait for the others next time. What I did not know was that all our instructions were live over the public address, and it caused some laughter in the stands. The real problem then arose, for as I called Set, the crews on either side of the Canadian crew set off on a false start. The procedure had to begin all over again, but Mike and I could not understand how that false start had occurred. As we came down from the start tower, a Scottish official who had been behind the Canadians, confirmed that their Cox had shouted Go, as I called Set. Not aware of this subterfuge until after the race was well underway, we could do nothing about it. Fortunately they did not medal, and finally admitted they had deliberately caused the false start. As a result of this chaotic affair, we brought in the simple start for all our domestic events, and took away from crews the ability to delay starts by raising hands during the last two minutes of the procedure which then came under the full control of the starter. Within a couple of years FISA had seen the sense of our changes, and brought them into the International Rules. Of course things have moved on since then, and now all major courses have electronic starting, and false starts are largely things of the past.

The Championships were held in Moscow in 1973, and I attended both as an umpire and as a journalist for the Nottingham Evening Post. We flew from Luton, but were delayed due to the time it took to open the front section of the plane, to allow the loading of all our boats. A great friend and distinguished rowing journalist, Desmond Hill, had just arrived home from a family holiday in the West Indies. He opened his mail and panicked feeling he would miss the flight, threw fresh clothes in a bag and high tailed it for Luton. He looked in a bad way, having not slept for 24hours, and slept little on our flight to Moscow. Arriving two hours late, we were deemed to have somehow missed our slot, and since the airport closed at midnight we had to circle for what seemed ages, before we were allowed to land. Our boats were unloaded and put on a trailer, but since at that stage we had no towing vehicle we had to leave it on the tarmac under the care of Jimmy Wallis our boatman. When we left for town, he was promptly arrested and locked in a small cell until his status could be established. He had bought one of those packets of three or four biscuits at Luton, and sat in his cell wondering how long he would have to make those biscuits last, for we were there at a time when our view of the Russian regime was not exactly warm and friendly. However all was sorted when the West Germans took their trailer out to the airport and brought Jimmy and our boats to the course.

We were taken to an old hotel The Centrali on Gorky Street in central Moscow, and in our exhausted state refused to be called at 8am, and certainly Desmond was not going to be roused without having a good nights rest. We came down for breakfast at about ten, but in common with some French Hotels, it did not run its own restaurant, and we traipsed next door where meals for the hotel were served. We were all still weary eyed and Desmond's generous features were still such that you could hardly see his eyes. As we sat at our table we were puzzled by rude noises coming from the waitresses who were setting out the tables for lunch. They were spreading clean white cloths on the tables, and then having filled their mouths with water, they sprayed the cloth in order to remove the creases. In out tired state, we all just collapsed with laughter at this improvised method of ironing out the creases in the linen. Our group of officials and wives were well chaperoned by a young girl, Violetta, whose English was excellent, but who had never been further than 25 miles from Moscow. When out of interest we enquired about travelling to Leningrad, she said it was not possible, for additional visas would be needed, indeed as a Russian she could not travel there without a permit. I could not help but gently probe her with questions about their way of life, and who could and who couldn't join the Communist Party. She indicated that only a few million were actual Party members, and when I mischievously pointed out that it was about the same percentage of the very rich that controlled all of us, she felt I was just pulling her leg. When we suggested that we sent her some books or magazines once we returned home, she thanked us for the idea but made clear she would not be allowed to receive them, and any acceptable books would have to be cleared for inclusion in their library. As the two weeks came to conclusion, we all agreed to invite her to join us for a farewell supper. During the meal, and not as a result of any serious political conversation, she leaned across to me and said "Mr Brandon-Bravo you have left me very confused".

The Moscow equivalent of W H Smith of Gorgy Street was a further illustration of how different their world was from ours. In any other capital city in the world, such shops would have at least a few newspapers from other countries, but not in Russia.

Indeed the only English language paper was a shortened version of the Morning Star. Their postcards gave us a chuckle and one was a picture of a family sitting around a long refectory style table, with a stern faced father at the head, mother at the other end, and a large bowl of something or other in the centre, waiting for its distribution. It was not the sort of holiday card ever seen back home, but we took a chance, added a message to my staff back home: "Workers of the world unite!" Surprise, surprise, it was delivered to the amusement of all.

Jim Railton who had been our National Coach, was then the Times correspondent and sat drafting an article on the Russian bid for what became the 1980 Olympics. He and other journalists had been given a rough time by their "guardians" during the World Student Games that preceded our Rowing Championships, and was in no mood to be diplomatic. Sally had come with me, and Jim passed his draft for her to proof-read. When she had read the last paragraph, she said that he could not file it, for the Russians were not daft and would know just what he meant. He had ended his piece with the comment that, since Russia, and therefore Moscow, had to have the Olympics sometime, better it was 1980, for 1984 would be singularly inappropriate! He said to hell with them, they can put me on the next plane home, I've had them up to here. Needless to say our embassy contacted him the following day and expressed their concern at his having filed his rather provocative piece. They did not pack him off home, but for the next ten days, he was followed by two little guys that had KGB written all over them.

Desmond ran into trouble again, for the Russians had designed the entrance to the stands through two pairs of glass doors, to reduce draught. Unfortunately they had used ordinary glass panes rather than thicker toughened glass, and had failed to put any markers on these pristine panels. Desmond promptly walked straight through one of the panels, and a shaft of pointed glass penetrated his generous rear end. We should have been sympathetic and not laughed, but the image of our friend lying on his tummy, with a Russian nurse stitching his backside, was just too hilarious to take seriously. He was a great sport and took the joshing in good spirit, and certainly brightened up our stay on what was a very drab occasion.

There was one service in Moscow that would never have survived in England. On the streets were drinking water "fountains" consisting of two compartments In one an upturned glass –yes a real one – which you pressed down to wash the glass, and another where you pressed to fill your glass with water. When finished the glass would bc returned to the washing compartment. I could not imagine such a system lasting for five minutes in any of our cities. Quite what the punishment would be on a vandal breaking the glass I shudder to think.

One further incident illustrated the kind of attitudes prevalent in Soviet Russia at that time, was when one of our group drew my attention to the fact that the Israeli delegate, Jonny Szabo, had had a rough time on arrival at the Moscow airport. They had gone through his bags with a toothcomb, confiscated the magazines he had with him, and generally made him feel both frightened and most unwelcome. From all accounts he had locked himself in his hotel room at the Rossia Hotel, and would not join the early meetings of delegates and officials. Sally and I obtained his room number and knocked on his door. His frightened response said it all, but we called out shalom and he let us in.

He had unstitched his Israeli blazer badge, so that if he did attend any gatherings, his identity would be hidden. He insisted I accepted his badge, and I still have it as a memento of the pressures some Jewish people still labour under. He was Hungarian by birth, and emigrated to Israel after the war ended, living in a suburb of Tel Aviv, returning occasionally to Budapest, though after what he had been through I found it difficult to understand why he felt he should visit "home". For him, the only survivor of his family following the holocaust, the Russian anti-Semitic attitudes must have hurt him deeply. When he retired, his son Eli took over the Israeli Federation's presidency, and our friendship continued for many years.

Our hotel had a receptionist on each floor, in addition to the main reception on the ground floor. I had arranged to file copy to Nottingham on a reverse charge payment, but after my first call, the phone rang and a voice said "Nottingham ten minutes". I took no notice since I did not expect to have to pay. However each time we left our room, the receptionist would rise from her desk and say "Nottingham ?" and I would say "Yes". To which she would say "You pay !" and I would wave my hand and say "No Nottingham Pay." This went on for about five days, when she was getting more desperate each time we left our floor. We had complained about our so called first class room, which had two single beds placed head to tail, there being insufficient room for them to be side by side. We had brought a rubber ball for the hand basin, but Sally was convinced we were under surveyance since we could not turn the radio off. When we were finally allocated a better room on a different floor, we packed our bags and as we stalked past the receptionist, she rose with a choked expression, but I waved her away, and to our surprise we heard no more about YOU PAY ! It was only when we were back in Nottingham that we found there was no reverse charge possible at that time, and so I do hope the poor receptionist did not end up in a gulag.

The autumn and winter is primarily taken up with long distance time trials or Head Races. They are held all over the country, wherever the available river is suitable, and ours in Nottingham boasts one of the biggest entries. However even though the stretch of river is long enough, the width demands that we run the event in three divisions. The only Head that can cope with a full entry in one division, is that held on the Thames, over the reverse Boat Race course at the end of March. There some 500 eights compete in what must be one of the biggest athletic one day events in the World. The sight of early crews racing down the centre of the river, whilst crews in the higher numbers are still paddling to the start up the sides, is a sight to behold. When you note the number of overseas crews, and the spread of home crews from all over the United Kingdom, you wonder why it has taken so long to dispel the public image of our sport that ties it solely to the Boat Race and the Royal Regatta. We have to thank Steve Redgrave for opening the public's eyes to the reality of our sport.

In truth I had enormous fun, double sculling with a guy called Mike Collier who still races in the Masters category at 82 years of age, or dropping into the odd coxed or coxless four, or pairing with either club-mates Kevin Bruton or Robin Haslam, and of course an eight whenever possible. In the early sixties, it was possible, particularly after Henley Royal, to put a crew together and do a bit of what was then described as pot hunting. On one such summer Barry Start and Pete Hubbard from the Britannia, Kevin Bruton and I formed a combined four that just clicked together, and with the driving force in the stroke seat from Pete, we had a great season with five or six wins throughout the provinces. I can't claim it was at the highest standard, but it was great fun. Added to that, I spent whatever time I could spare in coaching, and derived great satisfaction seeing crews under my care, collecting their winning trophies at regattas up and down the country. It was a great diversion from the pressures, first of business and factory management, and later during my time in Parliament. For me there was, and is, no greater participation sport.

When I left Parliament I returned to Rowing, and was approached by old colleagues who suggested I accept a nomination to be President of the Amateur Rowing Association. I was surprised and greatly honoured to be elected in 1993 and took on the Caversham Project which has played such a major part in the continuation, and indeed growth of our sport's world reputation, and is a chapter of its own later in the book.

The eight years of that Presidency could not have been more challenging or exciting, for it began with our sport's Gold medals in Barcelona, and ended with Steve's fifth Gold medal in Sydney. My first World Championship as President was at a course in Roudnice just outside Prague in 1993, when both Steve and Matthew, and the Searle brothers retained their titles, together with an outstanding win for our lightweight women, and a fantastic gold for Peter Haining in the lightweight men's sculls. Peter's win was a dramatic demonstration of skill, for leading with barely a hundred yards to go, he touched a buoy and lost his left scull. It seemed all over, yet somehow he reached out, reclaimed his scull and shot off after the Australian sculler who had taken over the lead, reclaimed the lead and a well deserved Gold. As I left the stands with the Associations executive chairman Di Ellis, I could only say, "What on earth are we expected to achieve next year!"

As always the International Federation held it's Congress before the opening of racing, and our official delegation to Congress was our Chairman Di Ellis, our International Manager Brian Armstrong, and me. I was delighted to draft an impassioned bid to have Mike Williams our own association's treasurer elected as the International Federation Treasurer. Being my first Congress as leader of our three "man" delegation, I wasn't sure how far to go with my presentation, but it was successful, and I had to chuckle when Dan Topolski came over said, "well done, it brought tears to my eyes".

The following year the Championships were in the USA in Indianapolis. The medals kept coming, but as a city, Indianapolis apart from the famous race track which we duly toured and received our certificate, was what we would disparagingly call a one horse town. Considering it was a metropolis of over one million people it had virtually nothing to commend it. A handful of restaurants, a tiny theatre, and a converted railway station providing some shops and cafes, and that was about it. When we expressed surprise, we were told that local folks simply didn't dine out in a way we take for granted in Europe and the UK, and that time after time, restaurants opened and closed in the absence of any demand. We were entertained by some British ex-pats working for Ely Lilley, and were staggered to find that their swimming pool was fenced off on the grounds that if a burglar fell in, they would be held responsible.

The Championships in 95 were at Tampere in Finland, but racing conditions on that lake, made the problems at Holme Pierrepont seemed petty by comparison. A thunderstorm created mayhem when the amount of rainwater on the stadium covers, caused them to collapse soaking the media center and spectators.

The Olympics in Atlanta followed in 1996, but instead of the racing being held on Stone Lake as planned in the USA submission, it was transferred some fifty miles away to

President British
Rowing (ARA)
1993-2001

Gainsville. Our team preparation was nearly fouled up, when someone, perhaps from Germany, tried to disrupt our planning by trying to spread the story that our chief coach Jurgen Grobler had been a member of Stazi in East Germany. Fortunately I still had contacts in Parliament, and a good friend in the Foreign Office had the story checked, and confirmed that people in many different careers, such as coaching in athletics, were for payment purposes, members of Stazi. I was assured there was nothing amiss and that we should ignore the innuendo and say nothing to Jurgen or any one else. Racing conditions were excellent, and being almost the first sport in the Olympic programme, we were all cheered when Steve and Matthew claimed gold in the pair. What no one had anticipated, was that theirs was the only Gold for GB in those games. We had one trip into Atlanta, and thankfully it was the day before the deranged guy set off a bomb in the City centre. Our women hit the headlines for laying down in protest in front of the bus due to take them from the village to the Rowing Lake, because the organisers had taken on drivers from all over the US, and many had absolutely no idea where any of the destinations were.

After the 1992 General Election, my old boss David Waddington had been made Governor of Bermuda, and had invited Sally and me to spend a few days with him there. The Atlanta Olympics offered an excellent chance to break our return trip to England. We stayed at the impressive Governors House, a classic colonial residence, with a wing of the property all to ourselves. The weather was gorgeous and the sunlight bright as we'd ever seen. We had a most elegant and distinguished "butler" to look after us. Standing at around six foot two or three, this black guy with crinkly grey hair could have made a fortune in films. Errol knocked on our door that first morning, and quietly asked Sally if madam would like him to draw the curtains. With her hands quickly over her eyes she said, "Thank you Errol, but please do it slowly". The Island had an annual cricket match between two of the villages, and the scene had to be seen to be believed. True they had a cricket pavilion, but all round the ground, the visitors had erected two tier private scaffolding grandstands, where from the upper tier they set builders chutes, so that the empty beer bottles were just tossed down the chute to bins at the base. Alongside the match was something of a fun-fair, and David told us that we would have to expect to lose a few dollars playing Crown and Anchor. The game is illegal at home, for the punters are not supposed to win, but win we did if only for a few dollars and a big laugh. It was also at a time when one of the Parties on the Island was pressing for independence, and felt that David would deny a vote on the issue. In fact he agreed, and the vote was lost, showing David's gamble had paid off. After four years he was ready to come home, but was asked to stay on until after the 1997 election so that an incoming government could appoint his replacement.

The Championships in 97 in D'Aiguebelette in the Savoy region of France, were overshadowed by the death of Princess Diana, just before the five days of racing began. We were aware that some single day events back home, were either being cancelled or delayed, but we took advice from Sport England and the Secretary of State, and were told not to withdraw the team, but to seek help from the organising committee in order that a race including a British crew would not clash with the planned funeral service back home. Di Ellis, Sally and I went shopping for black ribbon and a box of safety pins, and all British competitors wore them throughout racing. The organisers granted a minutes silence on the day of the funeral, and the Union Jack was raised only to half mast when the four won gold. The photo of the four, heads bowed, with black ribbons on their vests, featured prominently on the back page of the Sunday Times, and the press complimented our sport on the way we had handled that tragic situation.

Cologne followed in 1998, and St Catherine's in 99. Both events had problems with conditions. Cologne set deep between high banks seemed impervious to wind problems, but the finals had to be seeded based on semi-final times. Peter Haining, a double Gold Medalist, who had stepped up to the open rather than lightweight class, found himself placed in lane six after the semi-finals, and effectively had no chance in that disadvantaged lane in the final. That championship coincided with the Monica scandal in the USA. I could not help pulling the leg of my opposite number, the President of the US delegation, and asked him what was all the fuss about a cigar? He professed ignorance of the case, but said he would look into it and come back to us. He returned with the happy news that it was not an indictable offence since the cigar had not been Cuban.

The Canadian course appeared excellent and flat calm, but weed became a bit of a nightmare. Our women's lightweight pair had a ding dong neck and neck battle with the pair from the USA, but they picked up some weed at about the 1750 mark, and wobbled off line. They lost by a few feet, and the umpire inspecting their tiller, showed a bunch of weed, and raised a red flag indicating that until investigated further, the result should not stand. FISA called myself and the USA president to consider what should be done. The rules decreed that the Jury should consider the Umpires decision, but the Americans made clear they would appeal, and would continue to appeal all the way up to the FISA executive. This would have taken so much time, that the re-row, if that was the outcome, would have had to be held long after racing was complete. Taking advice from David Tanner and Di Ellis, I agreed that the case should go straight to the executive, and we would accept their verdict. I'm afraid TV won the day, and the result was allowed to stand, and I feel that our women were denied the justice of a re-row, for without the pick-up of weed they would have won that final.

The run-up and preparations for Sydney, just as had been the case prior to Atlanta, were almost derailed with the re-emergence of the phoney Stazi accusations against Jurgen. There were those, even within our sport, who regardless of the consequences wished me to seek the dismissal of Jurgen. I discussed it with

Di Ellis our executive chairman, and following personal meetings with Jurgen I made clear in a television interview that I believed in British Justice, and not trial by media innuendo, and closed down the story.

Our squad were magnificent in the Sydney Olympics, which will forever be remembered as the time Steve won his fifth Olympic Gold in a row. When we went through the security check that Saturday, the Oz on duty grabbed my arm and said, "We all over here want Steve to win his fifth". Our little group of association officers, were some 100metres from the finish line, and the buoys often distort your line of sight, so when the fours approached us, it did look as if the Italians were gaining on our four, and as they approached the finish both Sally and Di were almost in tears at the thought our four would be caught. When the line was crossed and the line of air bubbles indicated the Gold was ours, both of them cried even more, but this time for joy.

I took the Oz's good wishes in the spirit it was given, but I also knew that the Ozzies felt sure they would win the blue ribbon for the Eights the following day. To everyone's surprise, except the crew themselves, GB won that Blue Ribbon Event over a shattered Australian Eight. Our women also picked up their first Olympic medal, with Silver in the quads.

Obviously racing was our priority, but for me my role leading the British Delegation at the annual FISA congresses gave me great satisfaction, and on each occasion we did try to consult with key clubs and athletes, to ensure that our interests were protected. I took an early decision to ensure that our International Manager was always our third delegate, for our priority was always what was in the interests of our athletes, and he would know what was best for our squad.

Major changes were supposedly only to be taken at the Special Congress held in either the January or February following an Olympics, but occasionally some of the senior FISA officials tried to slip things onto the agenda of an ordinary

Congress. We always objected, since there would not have been any way of consulting prior to an Ordinary Congress. Kurt Nielson, a well respected international and coach, thought he could just propose the scrapping of some events, and accused me of being an interfering b***** politician, but I simply replied that I happen to think these things were for Congress, not him, however distinguished he thought himself to be. Similarly in Indianapolis the Americans proposed that women's lightweight four should be scrapped and replaced by quad. It might well have been the right thing to do, but since there had been no prior notice, Di and I objected, and made clear such changes had to be notified to Federations in good time before Congress. We took some criticism from both the USA and Canada, but in the end they agreed that these changes should be handled properly, for FISA had to recognise the rights of Congress, and not treat Federations as just rubber stamps.

Many of these difficult decisions arose as a result of pressure from the IOC each time a new sport was accepted into the Olympic programme, requiring established sports to reduce the number of athletes their sport could have, to make room for the new. At one such congress I had to say that established, first past the post sports, should not be penalised just to allow performances such as synchronized swimming, however attractive they were, to reduce the long established events such as Rowing. I felt such performances were more akin to the Hollywood stuff of Samuel Goldwyn and his star turn, Ester Williams. At a later Congress the executive accepted our suggestion that instead of snap decisions to scrap a class of rowing, a system that stated that if an event failed to have seven entries in three successive years, then, and only then, would that event be scrapped. We made the point that it was a simple case that if Federations wanted a particular event to remain in the programme, then they should enter and support it.

Perhaps our greatest success was my last Extraordinary Congress in Porto in February 2001 following the Sydney

Olympics. Our delegation went to Congress with five items we wished to press and achieved them all. One was that the Nations Cup which Italy ran for under 23s, and was to all intents and purposes, a World under 23s Championship in all but name but never designated as such. We proposed and achieved a timescale by which this event would be properly recognised and is now formally staged as the World Under 23 Championships.

But perhaps our best score was the proposal that whilst French and English would remain the two official languages of FISA, in all matters relating to the rules, procedures and their interpretation, English would prevail. When put to the vote every hand but one was raised in approval, the one against was our friends over the channel. Our delegation sat behind the Swiss and the Swedes, and they turned to me to query one point. They said "Martin in the English version you use sometimes Sex and sometimes Gender, what is the difference?" I thought for a moment and said, "well you can have sex but you can't have gender". They smiled in understanding and raised their hands in approval.

I passed any comments and points that needed to be raised to David Tanner when we came to dealing with the detailed section on drug testing and procedures. David did query with me one point since the English translation from the French version referred to the testing of either blood, urine, or gases. I said well they don't mean what you're thinking, and it appears that the French don't have a word for breath that distinguishes it from the other ! We got that quietly changed during lunch.

After the Athens Olympics, the Special Congress was held just outside Dubrovnik in February of 2005. My friend Douglas Calder who had a home in the Cayman Islands, had some years earlier signed himself up as the Islands FISA delegate, and also somehow got himself registered as it's IOC member. He asked whether Sally and I might be going, but since I had retired from the Association's Presidency I said we wouldn't be attending. He promptly suggested that Sally and I joined him and his wife

Debbie, and that I could be registered as a second Cayman Island delegate, which was sure to raise a few eyebrows, and perhaps a degree of consternation on the top table ! I agreed, and Douglas and I delayed our entry into the Congress Hall until the last moment, just to make a grand entry. In fairness, Douglas had been a great help at previous congresses, for being a lawyer was useful in ensuring that the text of any proposal at Congress was clear and unequivocal in interpretation.

In short, whilst it is right and proper that the plaudits go to our athletes who since 1984 have brought home Gold at every event since then, plus fistfuls of other medals both at Olympics, World, Under 23s, Junior and University Championships , for us lesser mortals there is great satisfaction in being associated with a great sport, and more than content to contribute in many other ways than just on the water.

CHAPTER 6

A HOLME PIERREPONT STORY

For some years from the late fifties and through the sixties, the Nottingham Rowing Clubs were looking for an alternative to the traditional regatta course which had run down-stream from the old Toll Bridge, round a fierce and unfair bend, to Trent Bridge. We tried a straight course from the Suspension Bridge, along the Victoria Embankment, to the Lady Bay Bridge, and also the reverse back upstream over that same course. Nothing really worked, though we managed, and the Regatta was always popular. Many of the trophies were outstanding examples of the 1800s, and the Gold Vase for fours became almost uninsurable. The Vase and the Turney Trophy, the latter an enormous and elaborate punch bowl, whilst still in the ownership of the Nottingham and Union R.C. are on permanent loan to the City and are on public display at the Council House. We have taken much the same security approach with the rest of the trophies, which are the property of the original Nottingham Rowing Club, now registered as NRC (1862) to distinguish it from the newcomers NRC(2007) who were once the Boat and Britannia Clubs. These are now on public display at County Hall along with NIR trophies held in trust by British Rowing. Both local Authorities insure the trophies under their Civic Silver insurances, and so are a good deal for the club, and British Rowing.

There was quite some publicity at the possibility that the Water Authority at that time, might consider dredging the straight stretch of water upstream of the Clifton Bridge, which would meet the sports needs, but the cost was prohibitive.

However back in 1968 I was fortunate to be elected to the Nottingham City Council, and at that time the City were developing the Colwick Park and Marina on the north bank of the Trent. I arranged to see the Chief Estates Officer, Mr Ned Evans, and we looked at the two planned sections of water in the park, which were to be separated by a narrow bund. I had hoped that the bund could be removed, and we'd be able to have at least a 1200m straight course on which to hold our regattas. Technically this became impossible because of the fall of the land for access for boats to the planned marina, and providing the second lake for general public recreation. This fall of course is why many find it difficult to believe that the course at Holme Pierrepont is nine feet higher at the boathouses, than at the start. So it is not only racing the 2000metres that makes it feel uphill !

Mr Evans however was good enough to recommend, and set up a meeting for me with his counterpart in the County Council. The Senior Officer there, Jack Long, was more than helpful and we looked at the then current and planned gravel workings. By happy coincidence Hoveringham Gravel had almost worked out the area of Holme Pierrepont, and were faced with the cost of a degree of restoration under the then planning conditions, plus their desire for further consents downstream in that area. I was asked what we needed, and not being greedy, stated that we just wanted a hole in the ground, about 2300 meters long, and the ability to set up temporary facilities so that a regatta could be held. He laughed and said he knew exactly what we needed, for he had been an officer in the Lea Valley, and was aware of the protracted debate that had gone on for years over the possibility of a course there.

A basic scheme was put together, and the then Conservative Leader of the Council, Cllr Mrs Anne Yates, not only gave approval, but enthusiastically began chasing funding for the

The Desolation
1969

project. Our biggest problem was with some of the then establishment at the ARA, for sadly some of the "elders" were less than enthusiastic about the possibility of a modern multi-lane course, and one in particular, the Chairman of Stewards John Garton, felt it would be the end of Henley Royal Regatta. It seems absurd now, but there had been schemes in the past that had just been kicked into the long grass, and few realised why there had been so little enthusiasm for a modern six lane course. At that time we were the only country in Europe apart from Bulgaria, without a six lane course, and only a very few ever had the chance to gain experience of multilane racing. Whilst granted that some were on lakes, Germany had fifteen at that time, and on top of all their other "advantages" that lack of experience goes a long way in explaining why so few medals came our way after the 1948 Olympics over the Henley Reach. All that changed rapidly in the years following the opening of the course.

The County Council put together a brochure and invited officers of the ARA to come to Nottingham for a presentation. They duly attended, and with funding coming from the Countryside Commission, Derelict Land Grant, Hoveringham Gravel – it was easy to twist their arm – John Players, and others, it was then put before the National Council. The debate in

Council was fraught to say the least, for the Lea Valley supporters argued that if there was to be a course, then it had to be in London ! It was typical of attitudes at that time, and the fact of Holme Pierrepont being in the centre of England, and was therefore reasonably accessible to everyone was conveniently dismissed. However the reality was that the Nottingham project could proceed almost at once, and with a single and willing Authority to deal with, completion on time and on budget, was assured. The Lea project was based on the timescale of gravel extraction, with many local authorities involved. When Council was faced with a Course now, against a Course in perhaps, and it was a big perhaps, ten years time, it ought to have been a no-brainer. When put to the vote however, Holme Pierrepont won by just a single vote, and only on the basis that it would have priority over the Lea in terms of timing. It is significant that twenty years later, Jeffrey Page wrote to me and said, that he had been wrong to have opposed at that time, and the decision taken then was right for British Rowing. It was a generous admission, and gave me a lot of pleasure to have received.

A committee was formed with Chris Davidge as Chairman, and officers of the Association, John Garton (with great reluctance), Freddie Page, Neil Thomas, Bill Clarke, Nick Nicholson and myself. Chris was FISA's technical director, and the specification was the then grade A, and the same specification as laid down for the 1972 Olympics in Munich. Apart from the Olympic grandstand, the Munich course cost between eight and nine million, whereas the Holme Pierrepont project was put together for 1.2 million, true value for money. We were lucky for at that time the construction industry was in recession and all the big boys fought over the tender to dig the course out. John Player paid for the finish tower, but political correctness decreed in time that their plaque should be removed, because attitudes to smoking had changed.

Much of the work was done in the winter, and conditions were a bit muddy. I used to visit to see progress most days, and on one occasion, my wife Sally and I drove down and entered the construction yard somewhere near where the new extension to the main building is now. We progressed slowly round the rough road where the slalom is now, and ran out of track when we turned to come down the south side. We halted faced with just a rough and somewhat muddy terrain, and were about to try to turn when a driver of one of the giant diggers, one which had an enormous central bucket and scraper, was having his snap (lunch) high up in the monster's cabin. He looked down, took pity on us and offered to see us back to the exit. He set himself up in front of us, dropped the great bucket/scraper, and proceeded slowly to the exit, flattening the rough soil making a useable road for us. He left us with a smile and a wave, and it is the only time I can say, a road had been made just for us !

Progress was swift, and we were able to have a trial run in 1971, with National Championships in 72 and formal opening by the Prime Minister Ted Heath in 73. Those early years were eye openers to say the least, and many, particularly novice and junior crews, were often overawed by the sheer size of the lake. For many, just looking back down the course from the start was most unsettling, and some of the early steering left umpires with much to do, for they too were learning a whole new approach to our sport. On one occasion a female cox burst into tears, having first tried to attach to lane 6, with No 1 in her bow slot, and then just could not attach. Chris Davidge was on duty with me at the time, and being a real gentleman, suggested I let her crew row, after all, the cox was just a little girl. No offense intended !

I umpired the coxed fours final at that first Championship, and with less than twenty or thirty yards to go to the finish, the Bedford crew, having been warned, clashed with the Thames RC crew who were clearly in the bronze medal position. Raising the white flag, I stopped the Bedford crew, and although a crew some way back crossed the line in third place, under the rules at that time, I awarded the medal to Thames. There was some consternation from both the disappointed fourth crew, and spectators, who had never seen that aspect of the rules before. After the race, Chris Davidge took me to one side, and said that what I had done was correct under ARA rules, but as I would be officiating at the championships in Copenhagen a few weeks later, I should know that FISA had by then changed the rules so that umpires could no longer decide the order of finish. It was just as well I knew, for I had the final of the single sculls, and whilst the winner was clear, the USA sculler was drifting into the lane of the local Danish favourite in the Silver Medal slot, and having been warned, I prayed he wouldn't touch the Dane, for a re-row whilst required under the rules, would have been most unfair. All was well and the Dane and the Yank, respectively got their Silver and Bronze medals.

One of our biggest problems arose from the structure of management of the facility, which was transferred by the County Council, as owners of the site, to the Sports Council, whose staffing arrangements employed people Monday to Friday with the weekends being overtime ! To compound that absurdity, they appointed Stan Dibley, known to all as Officer Dibbles, as manager. Whatever had been his background, it was a case of buggins' turn in spades, for his knowledge of our sport was minimal, and on one occasion we had to get him out of bed to open the gates to let crews enter the boat park.

We applied for a date for Nottingham International Regatta, feeling that the weekend before Henley Royal would make the trip for foreign crews, and particularly those from the USA and Canada, economic sense, with the likely knock on effect of increasing the overseas entry at the Royal. Once again certain members of the establishment were opposed, and I was absurdly accused of trying to wreck the Royal. At the FISA meeting in Denmark, our date was finally agreed, and as a result, the chairman of Stewards, John Garton who opposed our application, even suggested that he would increase the Henley course to three or four lanes, in order to both thwart our plans, and make the Royal even more attractive. It seems absurd now, but the facts are that from that time on, during the few years the Nottingham International was run, overseas entries for the Royal increased, and two of the Stewards, Angus Robertson and Hart Perry, had the foresight to market the two regattas in a package that offered two days racing in Nottingham, followed by racing at Henley for as many rounds as their standard and the draw would allow. There was a general feeling that NIR and the Royal should work together to make the most of the Robertson - Hart Perry package, but such was the antagonism from the top, the suggestion that we could arrange boat loans to cover both regattas, was only agreed providing I wasn't the appointed liaison contact.

Those half dozen years of the Nottingham International Regatta, were initially sponsored by Guinness as the major funder plus the two local authorities, Barclays Bank and Selincourt Ltd. The Guinness initiative was the brainchild of Dudley Bendall who became the Regatta Chairman in those early years. Those first three years brought teams from the USSR, East German, Hungary, Poland, Rumania, Bulgaria, Argentina, Australia, Japan, the United States and Canada, and many other Western European countries, in an event never before seen by the vast majority of our sport, outside the few who travelled to Championships abroad. However because the cost of funding the overseas crews could not be sustained, the last couple of years meant the overseas entry was effectively confined to the USA, Canada and Ireland who still welcomed the double event of NIR and the Royal. For whatever reason, the then team manager of the British team would not bring them to the International which further undermined the event, which would have at least created a four Nation Challenge. The International was then persuaded to change its date, and Bill Clark from the Association was deputed to run it as a more domestic event, accepting that we would lose the attendance of our few overseas friends unless we could find sponsorship to finance them. Inevitably this failed and the regattas coffers were decimated leaving us unlikely to be able to continue. The qualifying races for the Royal took the vacated pre-Henley weekend so there was no possibility of a return to that date, and effectively ended the Nottingham International. Fortunately entries at Henley Royal happily held up and in fact increased, indicating how short sighted those officers were, in seeking to avoid the creation of a British multilane course.

The International had its moments, on and off the water. When the Egyptians came, they rowed a borrowed eight to the start, and crashed bow on into the stages. Their sculler was disqualified for two false starts, and when he went down to Henley the following week, he was again disqualified as being late on the start !

If that first visit had been less than successful, they came a second time with a good friend of mine, Fayaz Yakkan, and were accompanied by one of their Ministers and his wife. I agreed to play host, and my wife, so that there would be no misunderstanding duly wore a beautiful gold Star of David,. Fayaz, who had become the International Governing Body's (FISA) the African Representative on the International Council, assured him of our hospitality and the minister duly came to our home in Barton in Fabis with his wife. They won one of the eights events, and being the first time they had ever won something abroad, the Ambassador invited the committee to the embassy in London. Being the diplomat that I am (!), I rang the embassy and wished to make it clear to the Ambassador's aid-de-camp, that my wife and I were Jewish, and we had no wish to cause him any embarrassment. To our surprise, the ambassador himself came to the telephone and insisted we came, which was even more surprising since he was the Brigadier Shazley, who in the 1971 war between Israel and Egypt, was reputed to have instructed his troops to take no prisoners. He was charming and hospitable, and when Sally and I were shown his great dinning room, and remarked that surely the beautiful ceiling frieze wasn't the original, and where was it kept, he smiled and said you only want to know where to plant your bomb.

The Eastern European countries were only able to come because of the funding we provided in those first few years, and came without any hard currency of their own. A Romanian crew were accompanied by a coach who spoke French, and with my schoolboy French I managed to look after their needs. We dug into our pot and gave each five pounds to spend in Nottingham, and they were staggered by the two shopping malls in the town centre, having nothing like it back home. They all bought women's tights, and when I expressed my surprise, the coach assured me that the tights would be worth a fortune back home. The Hungarian coach was a cheerful fellow, but his sole English was "yes, no, and gin and tonic!"

There was one sad incident with the Soviet team, who were accompanied by a very good looking lady called Valentina, from I assume, the KGB, at least she was politically in charge. She and Sally got on well, but when Sally remarked that surely what she was wearing had not been bought in Russia, she replied that she was a very privileged person, and that nothing, absolutely nothing, she was wearing was bought in Russia ! We had a small reception on the sectioned off area in the first floor dining room, and when we left, Sally realised she had left her umbrella behind the bar. When we returned, two of the Soviet crew and their Cox were putting bottles of booze from the bar into their kit bags. As politely as we could we indicated they should be put back, which they did, and we thought little more it. However we felt we should tell Valentina and indicating that no harm was done, and we considered the matter closed, but thought she should know so that no such incident would reoccur. We met up again at Henley, and expressed our hope that what had happened had not caused any problems. She replied that all was well, but the three crew members were already back in Moscow, and would not be allowed abroad again. It clearly was a different world to ours. On another occasion the Soviet coach had seen the display of fishing tackle on the far side of the course, and asked if we would be good enough to buy the lure and weight that was displayed in a small pack. Sally did so for the princely sum of about eighty pence. On delivery, he asked if she preferred Vodka or caviar as payment, and duly a half bottle of the real stuff was placed next to her at the hospitality table.

Holme Pierrepont hosted the 1975 World Championships, under the chairmanship of that same John Garton, with an excellent executive secretary in John Smith. The County Council were major sponsors, and we owed a great deal to the late Cllr Michael Cowan, who was not only the then Chairman of Finance, but carried enough clout to kick butt, (mostly Officer Dibbles') and ensure the site and its facilities could cope with the numbers of athletes and public who had never been seen before in our sport in the UK. When I found that the Chairman had not granted Michael Cowan full access to the course, I altered his badge with the necessary code letter, and was perhaps

Finished at last!

rightly called over the coals by the Chairman. I was unrepentant, for he knew the contribution Michael had made, and as I pointed out, I had to live with the consequences of his prejudices, whilst he could retire back to Henley. It was just one more notch on the stick of my clashes with Garton, but it was the unrelenting, and unreasoned objection to anything I tried to do, that was actually why I ended up in Parliament. I had attended a National Executive meeting one evening at Hammersmith, chaired by Garton and serviced by our recently appointed Executive Secretary David Lunn-Rockliffe. Without reason, I was subjected to a tirade of abuse from John Garton, who railed against this ignorant no-body from the Midlands. I left and as I arrived home two hours later I was clearly still angry. Sally said "You've had another row haven't you. Why don't you chuck it in and go back to local government where you're wanted and respected for what you do". David Lunn-Rockliffe phoned the following morning expressing his anger at what had happened, for there had been no reason or justification for John Garton's outburst. Against his plea that I should stay on the executive, I said I had had enough and he should accept my resignation with immediate effect. Within a couple of months a by-election was called for a City of Nottingham local council seat, and I was duly selected and elected in 1976.

The World Championships of 1986, followed the Commonwealth Games at Strathclyde three weeks earlier, and like the first, racing conditions were pretty good. However there was one big slip up when Thomi Keller, the FISA President, took a weather forecast far too seriously, and with little warning brought racing forward that day, such that racing was over by the time the TV and public had arrived. Thomi also made the fatal mistake of declaring that after a couple of false starts in the coxless fours, there would be no further false starts called. Unsurprisingly the German crew promptly jumped the start and led GB by about a half length, and held it to deny Dan Topolski's crew the Gold Medal.

There were, and are, many criticisms of the course, but subsequent developments at Docklands and Dorney Lake, have made most understand that we are an outside, open air sport, and it is almost impossible to provide an artificial course, particularly in Northern Europe, that will not from time to time, be less than fair, and sometimes un-rowable. The late Thomi Keller insisted all the trees were removed, and you know how tricky that can be with the environmental lobby. But in a clash of policy between Thomi and the environmental lobby, the outcome was inevitable, the trees went ! However it did mean that since the wind was either straight up, or straight down the course, it was usually fair to all, though of course there are times when there is a side wind, but it's not very often. This point has been underscored with the problems at the 2000meter course at Docklands, and even the splendid modern track at Dorney, with its now required separate access to the start, has problems with side wind, which sadly meant that the first International event, the 2006 World Cup Event, had to be seeded one to six based on the outcome of the semi-final times.

Still the three World Championships at Holme Pierrepont, one Junior and two Senior, raced in good conditions in late summer. It is a pity that so many of our regattas are held in the spring and early summer, when conditions are to say the least problematical. But even in the spring, for whatever reason, comes five or half past five each day, the weather usually calms, as if the course is saying, "why don't you race until eight or nine in the evening, and I'll be good, and you can complete your racing programme".

When Desmond Hill reluctantly brought the National Schools Regatta to Holme Pierrepont, he did not feel it would succeed there. However he was the first to acknowledge that it worked very well indeed, and it has grown to be the largest three day event in the Rowing Calendar. With plentiful affordable accommodation all around, plus on site accommodation for officials and others, it remains the venue of choice for the schools, particularly for those upcountry and Scottish Schools who would have to think very carefully at the cost of staying overnight at Docklands or Dorney. Sadly of all the regattas over the last forty years, the Schools have been the hardest hit by bad weather, but over those years of its existence we have not lost that many days racing. There was however one Saturday when racing was called off shortly after midday, only to find that as ever by five thirty, it was flat calm and racing could have continued until eight or eight thirty. It was said however that the schoolmasters would have wanted the little ones to be in bed by then! Those regattas enjoyed either the open travelling grandstands set up by Pym Berry of Burton and Tom Fisher of Trent Rowing Club on the back of his flat back lorries, or the double decker buses now enjoyed at the National Schools. The open stands, by far the greater fun, ran foul of the early days of "elf an safety"!

Following the grossly unfair GB selection process of 1968, proper trials were held at Holme Pierrepont from 1972 to 1976 under the Chairmanship of Michael Sweeney, who had been a victim of that flawed 1968 system that had denied his crew, and that of a coxed four from Poplar and Blackwell of their rightful place in the Games in Mexico City.

Likewise the National Championships, the University Championships and many other events, still come to Holme Pierrepont, and it is to be hoped that this National Centre that has served the sport so well, will continue to be supported for many years to come. Sadly it no longer meets the current Olympic specification, and whilst it could still stage Junior, University or Masters Championships, the biggest events, such as the World Cup Races, Senior and Olympic events will inevitably be bid for, and staged, at the fabulous Dorney Lake course, the site of the 2012 Olympic Regatta.

CHAPTER 7

A CAVERSHAM STORY.

Whilst I made no great shakes on the water, I did feel I could contribute best to the sport I loved, by seeing through yet another project like Holme Pierrepont, and help to establish a centre for the British Team at Caversham. Whilst Holme Pierrepont was used for trials and a fair amount of squad training, it was increasingly obvious that the demands of the British squad would never be adequately met until they had a dedicated facility of their own, and not subject to trying to fit in with the needs of the centre which had commercial bookings for most weekends during the year, and others wanting use that was incompatible with the squad's programme. Top athletes like Steve and Matthew, trained on the Henley Reach, as did most of the squad out of Leander.

Looking back on that earlier project at Holme Pierrepont, which took barely three years from concept to completion, the Caversham project was a hairy roller coaster of over ten years, with fears that it would never see an end to the problems constantly thrown up on the way.

In 1995, Brian Armstrong the International Manager, had submitted a paper as part of the Facilities Strategy for the ARA. It set out the need for a dedicated training facility in the Thames Valley, and it was subsequently put before the Sports Council for consideration. I had been elected National President in 1993, and later was asked to meet up with Brian and David Sherriff who owned the Thames and Kennett Marina on the possible site of a training course. David Sherriff had opened a marina there in 1970, and had long held the idea of a rowing course there. He discussed the possibility with Redland Lafarge in 1993, who were neighbouring land owners, and they decided to take over and seek to progress the project themselves. I was leaving Henley for that meeting when Arnie Zarach popped out of the Little White Hart to say hello, and what was I doing in Henley? When I told him of our planned meeting, he referred to the potential course as Leander's. Being ignorant at that time of the background, I did realise that there could be a problem, but it was a false alarm, for the committee of Leander were fully supportive from the outset, even if some active oarsmen at that club were less relaxed about the plans.

The outcome of that meeting with David Sherriff confirmed that Leander did use a lake by the marina, but not on any formal basis, and that Redland/Lafarge who had large gravel workings and a processing plant there, had ideas for a 2000metre course just 100 or so yards further north of the line of the present course. That course was dependant on Redland obtaining planning consent to build 200 homes in the northwest corner of the site, and they were prepared to put £2million from the profit of such a development as part funding of the course, with the balance dependant on a successful lottery application.

David Sherriff was certain that the South Oxfordshire District Council would not approve of Lafarge's application, for they feared that being attached to existing Reading housing, in no time at all, Reading would be seeking to extend its boundaries and seek authority over all or part of the area, and that was a risk the District Council would not take. A very helpful director of Redland/Lafarge, John Leivers, whilst he had been in the industry for many years, had never seen a 2000meter course, and he came up to Nottingham, and was quite taken aback at the sight of the Holme Pierrepont course.

In 1997 he and I made a presentation to the planning authority, and whilst sympathetic to our aims, the members confirmed that they would not risk the downside of a housing development on their site which had been set aside for recreational purposes.

As a result, Brian, Di Ellis, David Tanner and I went back to David, who reconfirmed his desire of handling the project himself, for he had already bought much of the land necessary to provide a 2000metre stretch for our sport, and Lafarge/Redland were willing to sell the necessary additional land, to complete the needs of the course, and allow David Sherriff to build a new marina at the western end of the area. His plan was to remove his headquarters which sat in what is now the middle of the course opposite the new boathouse and training centre, buy the remaining necessary pieces of land, and move his marina and headquarters to the western end of the site, where he could build a larger marina catering for more long-boats as well as the current cabin cruiser clients. He felt that so long as the Sports Council and Lottery funding would meet the bulk of the cost, his contribution, just as had been the case with Lafarge, would meet the match funding requirements of any application.

Armed with the broad outline of David Sherriff's scheme, Brian Armstrong, together with Derek Casey the then Chief Executive of the Sports Council and David Carpenter, met up for supper at my home in Nottingham, and there was general agreement that the project was do-able. However Derek Casey rightly made the point that however enthusiastic we were, our sport did not have the time or the expertise to see a project like this through, and whilst we had a reasonable idea of what it would cost, such projects always exceed budget, and the ARA were in no position to take such a risk. David Sherriff had generously offered to build the course for an agreed sum, and hand it over on completion to the ARA. Casey and Carpenter did not feel the Sports Council could underwrite the project this way, and in any case felt David's budget might not cover the inevitable unplanned costs. That judgment was confirmed since the final cost was more than double David's original estimate, mostly as a result of design changes and regulatory matters, plus changes of Sport England staffers over the ten years that could not have been anticipated. What Derek Casey did suggest, and I admit that both Brian and I were delighted to agree, that he, on behalf of Sports Council, should apply to the Secretary of State for what is known as a section 27 agreement, that would allow the Sports Council to take lottery money for such a project, in effect granting themselves the right to draw on such funding for a project of their own. It had a precedent with a scheme in Sheffield, so providing we put together a solid case, we had every chance of success. Drawing on his experience in these matters, particularly with his background as a previous International Manager, Brian Armstrong did a great job in putting together the case for the project, and was the key to the granting of the section 27 agreement.

In order to prove David's match funding contribution, an independent financial evaluation was carried out, and confirmed that there was no financial gain for him as a direct result of the proposed contract with Sports Council, and that his contribution was adequate to meet match funding requirements. That in later years, the new and larger marina he built at the western end of the site, might have become profitable for him, was not relevant to our project. As it turned out, there were so many changes to the approach to construction, unforeseen snags in land purchase and transfers, his costs were far greater than he had bargained for, and he subsequently had to sell the new marina.

With the granting of the Secretary of State's approval, an outline plan was put together, and a meeting with Brian and myself with the Chief Officer of the SODC Mr Butt, and another senior officer, Paula Fox, was arranged. They were clearly very supportive, and on their advice an outline planning application was prepared. For practical reasons, the application was submitted to SODC by David Sherriff as the major landowner involved. There were two major objections, one from the Sonning area who were concerned at the possible increase in traffic in an area already jammed at busy times in the day, but an even greater one from Eton College. They, who having had our support when they wished to create Dorney Lake, then sought to argue that they could offer the GB team all the facilities they needed, without building another course. A meeting was held with Rodney Watson their bursar who was the then chairman of the Dorney Lake Trust, and our team which included Di Ellis our Chairman, David Tanner, by then our International manager and others. With letters of support from some fairly distinguished old Etonians; the then Minister of State Kate Hoey; and other sportsmen and women, we finally made the Eton Authorities understand, that the training needs of the squad could never be met on a facility who's priority was the needs of the school and the minimum number of commercial bookings needed to try to match the costs of running such a large facility.

When the objections of the Sonning Parish were satisfied by writing into the application, that the facility was for training only, and no regattas would be held, the traffic objections were withdrawn. Likewise, though I suspect with some reluctance, Eton withdrew their objections and planning consent was granted

One other objection resurfaced quite late in the day, for there had always been the Department of Transport's aim for another river crossing. Theresa May the MP for the area south of the Thames put in a formal objection on the grounds that the Department of Transport should not have the option of a bridge, blocked by our facility. The usual discussions with departmental officials took place, and when it was clear that the presence of our course would not block a crossing, and that there were championship courses in the world with bridges straddling the course, Mrs May readily withdrew the Local Authority and Regional objections.

A trust was set up to act as the legal means by which the scheme could proceed, and which on completion would then lease the completed project to the ARA on a long lease. The sad thing was that by the time the trust was set up, Derek Casey the original CEO of Sports Council had left, and now what had become Sport England, had year by year, changed every officer who had been there at the start, and who had knowledge of the background of the project had left for other fields. We found ourselves dealing with officers who appeared to have no understanding of what had gone before, and failed, or refused, to recognise any moral obligation to our main sponsor David Sherriff, who had put enormous time and money into his long standing wish to do something great for our sport. Even worse, they looked on their dealings with him as purely a commercial matter, and he having agreed to assist them further in how they handled the financing of the project, found himself landed with an enormous tax bill for notional gains that he had never had. These new officers, just did not want to know, and left him with the bill, and a foul taste in his mouth, having genuinely tried to do the right thing by all of us. I very much regretted that we, the ARA, were in no position to fight his corner, caught between what we knew had been the original agreement, and effectively a new Sport England who made clear their attitude to what they now insisted was simply a commercial deal.

Sadly too, John Leivers retired from Lafarge, and his successor, just as with the changes at Sports England, felt no moral obligation to the project, and made abundantly clear his only concern was the commercial interests of Lafarge. This added greatly to costs, and caused no end of animosity between all parties.

We found too, that the Sailing and Canoe Clubs that had, what was understood at the time, casual use of the water, successfully claimed rights that in the end Sport England had to meet at considerable cost. Those clubs now have facilities as a result of the ARA project.

Such unintended costs inevitably reared their heads, and one of the biggest was the risk analysis. This great tome was supposed to cover every conceivable risk, but as I said to the consulting engineer, he'd left out the possibility that the San Andreas Fault under California, might just stretch across the Atlantic and wreck the course. He laughed and told me he did not feel he needed to go quite that far, but as I pointed out, he'd just about covered everything else. As necessary as risk assessments are, I cannot but feel that these things get out of hand with professionals covering their backs in case some totally and unlikely risk might come back and bite them.

At the scheme's later stages I left the trust so that more qualified members Brian Armstrong and Mike Hart could now get down to details, and Brian and the architect did a great job on the training centre. At the time we thought we had provided enough car park spaces, 60 minimum as required by the SODC, but as time has gone on, the squad has grown, and the use of the centre has exceeded all estimates.

It had been suggested that the lake be named after David Sherriff, but he turned that down, and at his request it was named after our two great Olympians, Steve and Matthew. The Boathouse now rightly bears his name, for without his vision nothing would have happened. The facility was formally opened in April 2006.

This is not, and cannot be the whole story, for there is much that David Sherriff would be entitled to add, and much of the great contribution that Brian Armstrong made is confidential within the constraints of his role within the Sports Council. I have no doubt either that Derek Casey and many other officers of what became Sport England would feel that much of their efforts were undercut, firstly by the change of Government, and then by the total overhaul of the structure of Sport England that came just at the time when we needed some stability and continuity with the people we were dealing with.

However when I look back at the rise in British Rowing after the creation of Holme Pierrepont, and the quantum leap since Caversham has opened, I can't help but feel proud of having been just a small part of these great projects.

CHAPTER 8

LIFE IN POLITICS

I'd been elected to the Nottingham City Council, then a unitary authority, in 1968, but Harold Wilson brought in a change of qualification rules, that meant since I lived just half a mile outside the City boundary, I could not defend my seat and I stood down in 1970. The Heath Government changed the rules back again, and I was re-elected in 1976, and further developed an interest in Housing, Estates Management and Public Transport. These sessions on a local authority gave me an insight as to what was possible, and what as an individual I could achieve or at least influence. This as I indicated earlier gave me the background and confidence to try for Parliament.

In the early seventies I had been rejected by the pre-1979 candidate selection process, which consisted of three people, with whom if your face didn't fit, that was it. The Party however agreed to let me fight the 1979 election as a local candidate, and Margaret Thatcher subsequently changed the system of candidate approval giving me a second chance to show what I could do. The new system was a two day event which gave candidates a real chance to shine, and of course expose any weaknesses to the team of sitting MPs and Party Officials, such that whatever the outcome you felt you had had a fairer deal than the previous star chamber system.

My selection for the new seat of Nottingham South, had been even more traumatic and stressful than usual, for often friends would be trying for the same seat, and you just had to take whatever the outcome, shake hands and move on. In this case a local senior Councillor had been appointed as the Party official

My first election campaign, 1968. I was elected to Nottingham City Council with Don and Doreen

to organise the three Nottingham selection panels that would ultimately hold their final meetings on three consecutive evenings. They would be in order of perceived winablity, South, followed by East, and then finally North. That Councillor, who had a considerable stake in who from the South constituency could attend, made it clear that although he had been a candidate in the past, he would not be putting his name forward this time, and hence was given the task of organising the panels.

Having done so, and almost at the last moment, he had his name added to the potential candidates for the Nottingham South. Having been instrumental in setting up the selection panel, it was clear he thought his selection was a shoe-in, but for whatever reason, and it certainly wasn't my selection performance, since I had a temperature of about 103, he didn't win the vote. There had been four candidates on the final list, and we sat in a back office wondering why it was taking so long to announce who had won. Having eliminated two of the four, it transpired that he and I had tied in the final vote, and the chairman, Gordon Craggs, understandably did not wish, as was his right, to cast a deciding vote. On advice from Shirley Stotter the senior area agent supervising the proceedings, the options facing the selection committee were set out. The option of delaying for two weeks to allow the full membership to select was rejected, since East and North would by then have chosen their candidates, and that would have been grossly unfair on the unselected candidate for South.

The meeting agreed to a break of ten or fifteen minutes to talk it through amongst themselves, and they decided that they would vote again, to see if the deadlock could be broken. Apparently I won by a clear majority, and the conduct of the meeting was confirmed by the area agent as fair and correct under the Party rules. The Saturday following my selection was a celebratory dinner at Nottinghamshire County Hall with the Rt. Hon Cecil Parkinson MP as the principle guest. It was meant to be a celebration of my opponent's selection for the most winnable of the Nottingham seats, and he sat on one side of Cecil, and his wife on the other. Needless to say, my wife and I were dismissed to the far corner of the banquet seating plan, but that was a small price to pay for what turned out to be the most exciting part of my life.

Such was my opponent's disappointment and anger at what he felt should have been a foregone conclusion, he endeavoured to have the decision overturned by the Central Party. The following three weeks were a nightmare of uncertainty, even though I should have been confident of the outcome, given the assurance by the Party Agent that the outcome was the clear will of the members of the panel, and that the rules of selection had been followed beyond challenge. He finally withdrew his appeal some three weeks later.

Turning up for my first day in 1983, Michael Latham, the member for Melton, took me under his wing and showed me around. We finished up somewhere in the bowels of the palace, and even he who had been a member for some years, admitted he was lost. I was allocated a hook in the cloakroom, and saw the little loop of ribbon that was supposed to allow me to hang up my sword. Just one of the idiosyncratic customs that make the mother of Parliaments so fascinating.

The Sergeant of Arms office handed me a key to a locker for my personal bits and pieces. Now anywhere else, the lockers would be in a normal sequence, but since the number of members had grown over the years, no one had considered sorting them out, and it became a case of "seek and ye shall find"; yet another amusing introduction to the House. I suppose the feeling was that if you were clever enough to get yourself elected, you could find your own way about! I did get myself a desk and a comfy chair in an office above the Chamber of the House, shared with three other colleagues, John Maples, Humphrey Malins and Andrew Hunter. It was a far cry from the facilities enjoyed by the present membership.

We all got along fine, but our secretaries had an impossible task, for five of them shared a single office, each with filing cabinets, typewriters and all the rest of the paraphernalia a secretary needed. The photocopier was in a corridor and shared by heaven knows how many secretaries, and it was a miracle anything was done in a reasonable time. Frankly from what I know now, the present lot don't know how fortunate they are! It wasn't long before I took the decision to scrap any secretarial services in Westminster, and set up an office in a barn conversion at our home in Barton, which until then had been the village hairdressing salon which my wife Sally ran.

When gathering up my office equipment ready to take back to Nottingham, I found that one of the secretaries worked for an old school colleague Nigel Spearing, a year ahead of me at school, and now the Labour member for Newham South. She was surrounded by boxes of mail, and I asked how on earth she could ever find anything. She smiled and said I should see the rest of the stuff at Nigel's home. Those were the conditions back in the eighties, and clearly the changes in the nineties and following were long overdue and necessary if members were to do a proper and efficient job on behalf of their constituents.

Back in Nottingham, I found a first class secretary in Dorothy Pearson, who's husband Peter was a Sergeant in the Nottingham Constabulary Vice Squad. She ran a tight ship, and we guaranteed to turn round correspondence within seven days, using a new small twin disc computer at the Westminster end, and one of the new fancy electronic typewriters at the Nottingham end. A computer with a laser printer came a couple of years later. Exchange by first class mail for letters for signing, and tapes for further correspondence, turned out to be much better that trying to run an office solely in Westminster. Dorothy was a gem, and I shudder to think how I could have managed without her. The allowance made it possible to take on an additional part time clerk, who transferred basic details of correspondence onto discs in another small computer. There was no such thing as internet or emails then, and for some colleagues, my little twin slot machine sitting on my desk was a matter of great interest.

Those stored details came in handy when plans to drive a dual carriageway though the Clifton Council Estate in my patch were published. Being the second largest Council Estate in England, it was a matter of major concern. I felt that at least every constituent on that estate, and the two small adjacent developments, who had been in contact with me on various matters in the preceding few years, were entitled to be given the facts, and I approached the Sergeant of Arms for permission to write to them. Back then there were strict controls on the use of Parliamentary stationary, and he was assured that I did not intend to write to all 12,000 households in that southern part of my constituency. On that assurance, he asked therefore how many I wished to write too, and I replied 5264, and if he wanted to check the figure, I would show him the details of correspondence on

Success at the 1983 General Election - Celebrating with the Armstrong-Jones brothers

my little desk computer. He expressed surprise, smiled, and gave me the required chitty to draw the stationary for the correspondence.

Dorothy wasn't just a good secretary, she was a first class personal assistant, and dealt with calls from constituents with great care and courtesy. It also gave us the occasional laugh. A lady called to tell us that her husband had died. Dorothy expressed her condolences and assured her that she would take her husband's name off the computer records, so she would not receive wrongly addressed letters in the future. "Oh no me duck" she said, "I only wanted to tell you that having been married to that b****** for forty years, at last I can vote Conservative." Sadly there were insufficient constituents like her came the election of 92.

Having taken a seat that was supposedly a Labour stronghold, and with no desire at fifty one years of age, to take on yet another mortgage, I booked myself in for three or four nights a week at the Carlton club. For largely business reasons, I had been a member of the Junior Carlton for some years, and enjoyed their political suppers, which gave me a chance to see and hear many of the senior parliamentarians in our Party. The most significant of these was Margaret Thatcher, who was the guest of the club barely three weeks after she had taken up the shadow portfolio for the Environment, following her years in Education. The chairman suggested to members that Mrs T might be allowed to speak to her old portfolio, since she couldn't have had enough time to absorb the complexities of the new. Not a bit of it she indicated, and we were treated to a bravura presentation of her new role, indicating to all that this was a very special lady. So it was no surprise to me when she had the courage to stand for, and win the leadership of the Party.

Shortly after her election as Party Leader, she came to Nottingham to meet the faithful gathered in the large Mecca Ballroom. Major Rook as the Federation Chairman accompanied Mrs T around one side of the ballroom, and I as Vice Chairman introduced Dennis around the opposite side. If any of us had any doubts as to the worthiness of our new Party Leader, they were dispelled that evening. Some time before the 1983 election, she came again to Nottingham and met all the regional candidates and their officers at Belvoir Castle. After that election all the new members and their spouses were invited to No 10 to be greeted by her. As she shook my hand, she said "didn't we have a great day at Belvoir Castle". Those small things underlined the incredible recall she had, and it was no surprise to realise her fantastic ability to absorb vast amounts of information, way beyond most of us lesser mortals.

After the merger with the senior Carlton Club, I had one big complaint when I found myself having to stay there three or more nights a week. The beds were awful! Sally suggested I ask the club secretary if I could provide my own bed, on the understanding that when I lost my seat, as was perhaps inevitable, the club could keep the bed. I thought he would be most offended, but no he was quite happy, and a new bed was installed. I therefore had the same room each night, and first call on that room. It gave the doorkeeper some difficulty with members who used it when I was not there, and who complained it was the only one where they got a good night's sleep!

Having been a local councillor for eight years, I wasn't particularly nervous about getting to my feet for a maiden speech, but wanted to see how things were done, and planned to wait for some time since there were so many new members following the landslide of the 1983 election. However listening to some of the new guys, I felt that delay might actually make that first hurdle seem higher and higher the longer I delayed, and so on week three I was called. I thought I had done reasonable well, until was grabbed by my whip Douglas Hogg, who apologised for not having caught me before I rose, to tell me that custom required that I should not be too political in a maiden speech. Too late, but at least the Speaker, Jack Weatherill, gave me a smile of good wishes when I left the chamber.

During my first week, Edward Du Cann, the then chairman of the 1922 committee collared me and asked what I hoped to achieve. I told him frankly, that at 51 years of age, and having won a traditional Labour seat, I was just happy just to be here, and that when I left the House, I'd hope to leave it at least with the respect of my peers. The 1922 committee, held on a Thursday afternoon, was I'm afraid something of a joke with some members, for at the first meeting we were told that the meeting was confidential, and should not be reported outside. Driving back to Nottingham that evening, I listened with amazement to an almost verbatim report on what had transpired. It turned out that a few members, or "rentaquotes" as they were known, cheerfully breeched that understanding for the dubious publicity they achieved. At fifty one, it was presumed that I was the father of the new intake, indeed the Guardian suggested that

I was old enough to be the father of some of the intake. This myth was sustained until Stefan Terlezki, affectionately known as our Ukrainian Member for Cardiff, owned up to be a year older than me.

One perhaps small thing that illustrates the changing world we live in, was an evening when the Prime Minister arranged a meeting with a couple of dozen new members at a club near the House. After the formalities and a few drinks, she reminded us that Kenneth Clarke would be winding up the debate that evening. Apart from Ken being a friend and my local MP, most wanted to hear him, and we all walked back, unchallenged, to the Commons, with Mrs T chatting away with colleagues. Could that happen now, whoever was in government?

Given a hectic General Election, the settling in to a new life, the excitement and fascination of those first few weeks in Parliament, and trying to establish decent office facilities, the Summer break was most welcome. It happened also to be Sally's 40th Birthday, and we went to stay with one of her school friends who had married a Canadian professor at Trent University in Peterborough Ontario. We stayed one night in Toronto before our friends came to pick us up, and stopped off at a deli to try some bagels and pastrami. The waitress was a student, who promptly asked if we wouldn't prefer a Kaiser. I said the only Kaiser I knew of was the guy that started the First World War, but the student reacted as if she'd never heard of the event, and said. "Let me get you one, I'll pay". It turned out to be a bread roll sprinkled with sesame seeds and stuffed with about twenty thin slices pastrami. Welcome to the diet conscious North America.

John and Anita Earnshaw, arranged for us to visit the local Provincial Parliament, and to meet their National Member Mr Bill Dom in Ottawa He was amazed that we had paid our own fare to come to Canada, indicating that so long as it was Air Canada, he could fly anywhere for free. Given his palatial office accommodation and staffing, I had to ask what he was allowed

A briefing in Belize with Sir Geoffry Finsberg, Sir Nicholas Bonsor and John Wilkinson

in expenses on top of his salary. I recall he had then in 1983, a budget of $250,000, plus four free publicity letters to each of his constituents per year. I asked given that kind of back-up that was unheard of back home, how could he possibly lose the seat. He simply replied "with difficulty".

Whilst we were in Canada, the Cecil Parkinson affair hit the headlines, and having sat in on a session in the Ottawa Parliament, we went out to dinner in a Japanese Restaurant, sitting round a large steel "table" on which the food was cooked and served. We found ourselves sitting with a man and a young lady, who introduced himself as one of the Members of the Canadian Parliament and his secretary. Given the "affair" back home, we tried very hard to keep straight faces.

At the Provincial Parliamentary session, Sally and I sat in the special gallery, and were welcomed publicly by the Speaker. A motion was put, and being challenged caused a vote. As expected the division bell rang and a flunkey came up to the gallery, and requested we joined the Speaker for coffee in his rooms behind the chair. Puzzled by the long delay, the Speaker pointed out that sometime back members had complained that they were unable to attend votes within the kind of eight minute rule that we had back home in Westminster. The Parties therefore had agreed that the bell would ring until the chief whips of the three or four parties in their House, were content that their members were present and the vote could be taken. They should have known that some awkward s** would see this as an opportunity to disrupt or delay proceedings, and allow the bell to ring and ring. Ours only rang for twenty five minutes, but the record had been fourteen days, with all but the bell in the main chamber having been blocked off before it drove everyone crazy. I gather they have changed back to a more reasonable time limit.

At home, the criticism of our PMQs is often that Prime Ministers never answer the questions, but Pierre Trudeau took this to a new level. When a member rose during their PMQs in the Ottawa Parliament to ask whether the prime Minster would comment on something or other, he simply rose and said Non ! I've yet to see any of our PMs be quite so dismissive.

Early on I found myself on the standing committee dealing with a Housing Bill, and when it reached the third reading on the floor of the chamber I was called at just before ten o'clock on a Thursday evening. As I rose to say my piece, my whip Douglas Hogg dropped onto the bench in front of me, and held up a card saying "The Scots want to catch the 10.30". I took the hint, made some feeble comment and sat down. Needless to say Simon Hughes ignored the courtesy and rose to continue the debate.

Eighteen months on I was delighted to be asked by John Patten, the then Minister of State for Housing, to be his PPS. I did express surprise, for at my age I did not expect anything more than to work as a backbencher for my constituents, for whatever time the electorate allowed me. John was very clear; with my background in local government, and knowing that our

City had been a Housing Authority, I could be of real assistance, and not just the proverbial bag carrier. This was at a time when "Yes Minister" was all the rage, and at our first morning meeting with the rest of the team of civil servants, John said "what am I saying today". I stifled a laugh for it was the television programme writ large.

I dined most nights in the House, but occasionally walked back to the club for supper, before returning for the debate and vote later that night. On one occasion Michael Latham and I planned to take such a break, when it was clear that the second debate at 7 o'clock was of special interest to East Midland members, and we decided to stay. It was most fortuitous, for at 8 o'clock a bomb exploded at the club badly injuring a doorman and a member. I was PPS to David Waddington the Home Secretary at that time, and he gave me bed and board for the first week, and my colleague Michael Knowles did the same for week two, by which time I was able to return to the club to collect my belongings. No-one died directly as a result of the explosion, but sadly Lord Donald Kaberry, a really gentle giant of a man who had often joined us lesser mortals for breakfast , died within six months of the incident, and it was felt his death was as a result of the injuries received at the time.

The House voting arrangements undoubtedly puzzle many of the public, but those fifteen minutes going through the lobbies, often gave you the chance to buttonhole a minister, who would be willing to spare three or four minutes in the lobby, rather than having to set up a formal meeting in his Ministry wasting his and officials time. Often you might contact a minister's PPS and ask if the minister would be voting that evening, and could he spare a few moments in the lobby. You therefore often saw ministers sitting on the side benches chatting to a colleague before moving to register their vote with the clerks.

The strangest and intriguing vote for me was on the fluoridisation of water, where the main speaker opposing the bill was Ivan Lawrence. We were in standing committee considering another Bill, and popped up and down stairs as each vote was called. My home City of Nottingham was firmly against fluoridisation, and I was voting accordingly. Lennox Boyd was our whip and remarked that I was consistently voting against him. I said it was a free vote, and I would continue to do so. It was already late at night, and Lennox suggested I went back to the club, have a rest, and come back in the early morning. I walked back through St James Park to the club, showered, had around two hours sleep, and arrived back at the House four hours later, just as the voting bell rang at the end of Lawrence's over four hour speech. Lennox did not know whether to laugh or cry, but I hadn't missed a single vote against that bill.

A more amusing outcome of a bill was whilst I was PPS in the Home Office, and Douglas Hurd was taking an amendment to our licensing laws through the House. Whilst the majority of members were in favour of the changes, there were a number of very vocal members opposed to any change, but finally agreed to support the Bill so long as the constraints on Sunday drinking remained untouched. With this undertaking given, it went though the Commons without too much difficulty, and was then sent up to the Lords, where our Minister of State was a wonderful guy, the Lord Robin Ferrers. At the usual morning "prayers" in the department around nine o'clock the morning after the Lords had, contrary to the promise, voted for an extra hour drinking at Sunday lunchtime, Lord Ferrers came in when most of the team were already sitting round the table. Lord Harmer Nicholls who had been the member for Peterborough and famous for holding the seat with single figure majorities, had proposed that amendment to the Bill. Lord Ferrers grabbed me before he joined the group, and from his great height of some six foot four or more, said "Martin I did say 'not content', I assure you I did, but it wasn't heard and the vote was carried. What will Douglas do?" I said he wouldn't get hung, but as we joined the group round the table, there was general laughter and slapping of the table. Happily no one in the Commons attempted to overturn the Lords vote, and when we go out now for Sunday lunch we can enjoy an extra hour of relaxed drinking. For Lord Ferrers it was a source of great satisfaction and delight, for he received a letter from someone who assured him that forever on a Sunday when he took his family out to lunch, they would raise a toast the The Lord Ferrers.

In my nine years in the House I was fortunate to have been successful in two ballots for private members bills, and one to have choice of a Friday morning debate. The first Bill in March 1990, dealt with certain transport matters that all sides of the House were happy to support. One clause dealt with safety matters at night, for a famous rowing colleague had recently been killed cycling into the back of an unlit skip parked in the road, with no other lighting to warn of the danger. It passed all stages, and was given a fair wind and their blessing from the Labour front bench that final Friday morning. I was greatly angered when Andrew Bennett, the Labour member for Denton and Reddish called a vote knowing that there would be insufficient members present to see the bill through. He assured me he supported my Bill, and that it would in the future get through, but he was apparently angry that there would not be enough time left for a private member's bill further down on the list that morning, and it was his way of protesting. Happily it ultimately reached the statute book the following session of Parliament, but under the name of Bill Cash who did not have the courtesy to recognise the work done by colleagues in that previous session.

The other Bill in December 1991, near the end of my time in the House, arose from the dreadful case of child abuse in some children's homes in Leicestershire, some twenty or so years earlier. What struck me as grossly unjust, was that a perfectly innocent member of the House was referred to in the trial, and who could not in law defend himself without being held in contempt of court. As I assume would many members, they would have occasionally offered hospitality for an evening meal, away from a Council Care Home, to some of these children in their constituencies, and one or two made clear that if they could be faced with the suspicion raised in that trial, they would not risk such censure ever again. In addition, the children, now adults, were named, and many had put their traumas behind them, moved on, married and had families. They too had no redress, and so with the help of civil servants in the Home Office, a bill was put together, that gave lifelong anonymity to young persons affected in this way. Being a private members bill, it took time to get through all stages, and I found myself at the bar of their Lordship's House for it's final stage, barely a couple of weeks before the 1992 election, and I feared that one of the press barons would cause a delay and scupper the measure on grounds of freedom of the press. Happily he backed down, and I was proud to have been able to do some small thing for those abused children.

My Friday morning slot was devoted to Housing matters, the benefits of the Right to Buy, the unfairness of housing allocations, and the manner in which those who knew how to

With a UK delegation meeting
Israeli President Itzak Shamir

work the rules, claimed priority over those who played fair, and who often in my view were more deserving. I had a number of cases where a couple wanted to marry and sought a Council House, to be told "well get pregnant and you'll go to the top of the list". This was not what any of them wanted to do, but illustrated just how so called modern thinking was degrading society. The earlier Housing Act had given Local Authorities the right to declare that a tenant having been evicted for unreasonable and prolonged misbehaviour, could be said to have made themselves homeless, and therefore Local Authorities were not legally required to re-house them. Sadly they never used that sanction, the trouble makers knew they wouldn't, and therefore almost to this day, the problem of anti-social behaviour on housing estates remains unresolved. The worst and saddest case on my patch was a single young mother with many boyfriends, who had been allocated a house in a quiet cul-de-sac. After months of trouble she was finally evicted, but the Council felt they had to re-house her. With two small children that would have seemed the right thing to do, but lo and behold, some idiot in the Housing Department allocated her back to the same house from which she had been evicted. She arranged a celebration party, which ended in fire, and her two little children were burned to death.

Our Labour City Council had fought tooth and nail to block the Right to Buy, but, the Clifton Estate of some 9000 properties, originally with either black or dark green doors, and all having the same depressing aspect, steadily changed both its image, and the conduct of it's residents. It had a terrible reputation, made worse by the conduct of the pupils at a central comprehensive school. During the three day week in 1973, I was giving a lift to three or four of our staff who lived on the estate, and they were chatting about how the problems of the school and the estate were being exaggerated. Oh said one, there was the time when some of the kids stuffed mattresses down the sewers causing one hell of a stink ! Then again, they had thrown the music master out of a window, happily on the ground floor, and one did admit that her son had had the sleeve of his jacket ripped out. I smiled and said, if that's meant to be acceptable behaviour, heaven help the future for those living on the estate. All that has changed, new garden walls, porticos, bay windows, rendering, and so driving now round the Clifton Estate, I'm proud to have been part of bringing about that change.

In the mid-eighties unemployment was unacceptably high, and although the statistics based on travel to work areas did not indicate that Nottingham City was that much worse than many other cities, my local colleagues and I knew that the wide travel to work method used in producing the statistics, hid the true state of unemployment within Nottingham City, as I was sure was true in other similar cities. Richard Ottoway, Michael Knowles and I went to see the Secretary of State Lord Young, and his deputy the Minister of State, Kenneth Clarke, our own local Nottinghamshire, Rushcliffe member. At the time, there was a vast area in my patch taken up by disused railway lines and sidings, which had been partly used by the power station, and coal mine, both by then long gone. Efforts had been made in the past to get British Rail to release the land for much needed development, but always they used the excuse that they might need the lines some day, and like many public sector bodies never considered sensible recycling of their tied up assets. Kenneth knew the area well and backed our case for what the Americans call a real estate method of regeneration. Lord Young took up the project and British Rail backed down and divested themselves of the land which rapidly became what is now called the Queens Industrial estate, and employs many thousands more than ever worked either at the power station or the Wilford/Clifton mine.

Later when we returned to the question of unemployment, we obtained agreement from Michael Howard, to fund some research by Trent Polytechnic into the pepper pot effect of unemployment within the City, which showed one percent in some areas, and 40 percent in others. Sadly when the report was completed, we had to face the fact that in one or two areas of very high unemployment, far too many were simply unemployable, and that situation is still with us twenty five years on.

After the 1987 election, I went with John Patten, then Minister of State, to the Home Office. Douglas Hurd was Home Secretary, and was faced with a two part report, resulting from a case in Scotland, that had been commissioned to examine apparent War Crimes committed abroad by people now resident as citizens, or having been granted the right to remain, in the United Kingdom. The report by Sir Thomas Hetherington and William Chalmers was in two parts. The first part set out, without names, the broad picture of what was being alleged, and the second was confidential to just the very top Cabinet Ministers, being evidence that might be used should any person subsequently be charged, and therefore would have been prejudicial if made public. Their main recommendation was very clear, that "legislation should be introduced to give British Courts jurisdiction over acts of murder and manslaughter committed as war crimes, in Germany or German occupied territory during the period of the Second World War by persons who are now British citizens or resident in the United Kingdom". Douglas's comment was, and was repeated on the floor of the chamber, that having read the evidence collected, he could do no other than bring a Bill to the House. Many sought to argue that The War Crimes Bill would either be retrospective legislation, or that witnesses would be too old to be credible. Before the Bill started its journey, Douglas moved to the Foreign Office, and David Waddington became Home Secretary. I was honoured to be asked to move up and be his PPS, and I went with John Patten's blessing, and as a result sat with David throughout the passage of the Bill. There were some excellent speeches from many members, some who had good cause to see that at last justice would be done, and some who were shameful in the dismissive manner in which they sought to oppose. Those who argued that it was retrospective, would not accept that all the Bill sought to do, was to grant jurisdiction to British Courts, to address crimes that would have been crimes under British Law at that time they were committed, and would have been juridical had they been committed by a person subject to British Law. It was not seeking to make criminal an act that would not have been criminal at that time.

Many of the names somehow entered the public domain, and I found to my horror that I had one such suspect in my constituency. I was approached by the local press to obtain my opinion, and I arranged to visit a Mr Derzinskas, a man now in his seventies, who agreed to see me, and allow a journalist to be present. He was Lithuanian, agreed he was who it was alleged he was, agreed he lived in the village named, agreed that the Jewish women were taken away, to where he knew not, and that the men and boys were lined up and shot. He said he was there at the time, but he hadn't been involved. When we left, I asked the journalist what he thought. Frankly he said he was guilty out of his own mouth, but I said I was sure that the editor would not allow him to write it up, and that proved to be the case. Personally I felt sick, yet I also knew that if he wasn't charged, then for the rest of his days he would be waiting for the knock on the door, a knock that had terrified millions of Jews and other minorities, during the reign of Nazi Germany.

I expressed my view to David Waddington, that whether anyone would ultimately face trial, was almost irrelevant, but the Bill was important for if the British Parliament simply shut it's eyes to the horrors and did nothing, we would not be able to hold up our heads again. We also recognised that if the Bill left the commons with only a small majority, their Lordships might throw it out, but as it turned out, it was carried by a massive majority, and a credit to our sense of justice.

I had approached Greville Janner, who was a member of the Jewish Board of Guardians and he had agreed not to speak during the earlier stages of the Bill, persuaded on the grounds that we did not want this to be just a Bill about the Jewish Holocaust, but to cover all the atrocities committed during WW11. He however felt duly bound to speak on the Third Reading, and during his speech he referred to the fact that he had lost half his family in the Holocaust. Neil Hamilton sitting just a few feet from me, remarked loudly "The wrong half". Greville didn't hear, which was just as well, and he carried on. Because Hamilton had made his remarks from a seated position, Hansard was not obliged to record his outrageous comment, and did not do so. A couple of weeks later, Mark Lennox-Boyd who was Mrs Ts PPS approached me and indicated that she had received a letter from a constituent to whom Hamilton's remarks had been reported, and would she enquire if it was true, and what action might be taken. Mark wanted to know if I had heard it, and I confirmed I had, since I had been in the Chamber throughout the debate, as had David Waddington. "Oh gosh I can't just tell her that, can you confirm it with any others"? I agreed to seek out a few members who had been in the Chamber on our side at the time, and duly reported back, confirming my original statement. "Oh dear," he said, "How am I going to tell her." I simply said this is up to you, but better she knows the truth, than the matter is ignored and might surface again in the future. Whether Mark told her, I don't know, but it confirmed my worse fears that we were reaching the point where members only told the PM what they felt she wanted to hear. Sadly that's a problem facing all long term Prime Ministers, and probably contributed to her sad downfall.

As expected there was considerable opposition in the Lords, again on grounds of retrospective legislation, but also on the grounds of credibility of witnesses. Even with the Bill making clear that the rules of evidence and procedures were absolutely in accord with current legal practice, there were still those who objected, and their reasons were a matter for their consciences. Standing at the bar of their House during the debate, I did not know whether to laugh or cry at the sight of a peer in his mid nineties, arguing that witnesses would be too old to be credible!

The Hong Kong dilemma surfaced and was addressed in the British Nationality (Hong Kong) Act in 1990 when Douglas was Home Secretary, and the House accepted that whilst most Hong Kong citizens held British Dependent Territory Citizen Passports, they did not cover full citizenship and therefore no right to come to and reside in the UK. These passports at least gave such holders, a document that allowed them to travel anywhere in the world. The view was taken that it would be impossible to issue a possible 3.25 million passports to these holders, even if most would not seek to exercise that right of settlement. A figure, however arrived at, was chosen at fifty thousand, which it was believed would certainly cover all priority persons. As ever, since they did not have to make these difficult decisions and enjoyed the freedom of being in opposition, the Lib/Dem leader Paddy Ashdown demanded unsuccessfully, we grant passports to all residents in Hong Kong.

For whatever reason, since I was PPS in the office and with Home Office approval, I accepted an invitation from the Hong Kong Government to visit the dependency, and test the water so to speak. I was offered first class travel and accommodation, but if I wished to take Sally, would I accept business class? Avoiding the expected handbag, I accepted on behalf of us both! We met the Governor and various groups of lawyers and journalists, and whilst these interest groups where not shy in special pleading, I had to make clear, that whilst I could note their concerns and ensure that all views were reported back to the Home Secretary, as a humble PPS I was only the messenger, On one session, there were so many journalists wanting an interview, that Sally had to line them up in a queue outside our hotel room, and as it turned out, I avoided putting my inexperienced foot in it, and completed my task without mishap. We were treated to one very special treat, a helicopter flight over Hong Kong and the territories, and the dive back over the racecourse was quite spectacular.

Being in the Home Office had it's downsides as well being a fascinating experience, for we began to get threats from an IRA cell in Mansfield - North Nottinghamshire - and my concern was for my family. Of all the issues I had been involved in, I had promised never to be involved in Irish affairs, but non the less it meant we had to install all night security lighting around the house. We went out one Saturday night at about 7.30, returning at around 11, and Sally noticed a parcel pressed into the corner of our front door. It had not been there when we left, and there were no visible labels on the top and two sides that were visible. Sally insisted we called the police, who having inspected, could not discern any sender and decided to call out the bomb squad. Around 2.30am the army arrived with a special van, and a robot bomb disposal machine. We had to get our neighbours out of bed, and the small crowd gathered around the van and on a small TV watched the robot slowly crawl up our garden path, to face the brown paper wrapped parcel. Having inspected the parcel through the TV the officer in charge decided he would have to blow it up. The robot gun used something like a champagne plastic cork and compressed water, and the parcel exploded. We had just had the front door revarnished, and the contents of the parcel which turned out to be leaflets from the Department of the Environment, became a shower of confetti which stuck in tiny bits all over the door. It was a small price to pay for our safety, and our neighbours had a great night out !

My most enjoyable task was as a member of the Transport Bill in 1985 under Sir David Mitchell the minister of state at the department of transport. Fundamentally the Bill deregulated the operation of buses, and was the logical extension to the deregulation of the long distance coaches some few years earlier. For me, this was meat and two veg, applying practical common sense rather than politics, but of course Labour opposed it tooth and nail. Our City transport in Nottingham was a case in point, for it was run by Councillors, in the interest of Councillors in so far as if they wanted a bus to run down such and such a street, it would do so irrespective of any sensible justification. It ran at an ever increasing loss, and whilst most of the buses were old, Labour sought to argue that there would then be little or no new investment, and that it would be only a matter of time when there would be a terrible accident with a steering wheel coming away in a driver's hand.

I got myself onto the standing committee dealing with the Bill, and was proud to be told by David Mitchell that I probably knew more about the Bill than any other member, and had to take one of his consultation meetings for him. Our County Council also opposed the bill, arguing that they would lose all their rural services. As it happens, when all the commercial bids were in, and the "socially desirable" routes went out to tender, the County found that all their existing routes were covered and that they had a saving of half a million pounds. There were many who opposed it out of political prejudice, and some out of total ignorance. One non-constituent who wrote to me complaining that living in the country they did not have a bus or any other public transport, and the Bus Bill would be a disaster for her. I had to reply that if she didn't have a bus now, I could not see how the bus Bill could possible make matters worse.

The system was also unfair on our senior citizens, for there were differing schemes of concessionary fares in the Districts around and within the City. Where there was more than one provider on a route, only the City Transport would offer concession rides to City OAPs and only within the City. It meant that a senior citizen had to wait at a stop until a City Transport bus came by, so that he or she could use their pass, but if you did not live in the city you might have to pay if their District did not have some sort of arrangement with the City. I put down an amendment in committee, seeking to give all senior citizens living in the area covered by the transport arrangements, equal rights, and that any operator in that area, had to offer those same agreed concessions I am no legal draughtsman, and was asked that if I would withdraw my amendment, the Minister promised that a clause to meet my aim would be tabled at the report stage. I was justly proud, when the Secretary of State Nicholas Ridley rose to propose what he called the Brandon-Bravo clauses to give our senior citizens exactly what I had wanted. I don't claim it has all been sweetness and light ever since, for with an ageing population the cost of this provision is bearing hard on Local Authorities, but I still believe it was, and is, the right thing to have done.

As much as I enjoyed the jousting in the Chamber, I enjoyed my constituency work even more. As soon as I was elected, I bought an old caravan, cleaned it up, had a large banner displaying my constituency, who I was, and set up "surgery" each Friday afternoon or Saturday morning in the various shopping centres throughout the constituency. If I'd any doubts as to the worth whileness of the exercise, they were dispelled when I heard a passing resident say "The Labour Member never did this". I gave priority to those who had arranged an appointment, but set out a row of chairs outside the caravan, and if folks were prepared to wait, I'd see them. It certainly made the effort worth while.

In the winter I used the various libraries, and one winter occasion illustrated that you can never take a voter for granted. A probation officer asked if I would see a constituent who had foolishly wound his gas meter the wrong way, and was faced with a bill he couldn't pay. Whilst pointing out that it was a criminal act, I would still see him. He turned out to be a giant Rasta, who turned up in a most aggressive mood. I was pretty sharp with him, and using a short well known expletive, told him if he wanted my help, to stop mouthing off, and sit down and tell me what had happened. I can't recall what I did to help, but many months later at the 1987 election I was at a temporary polling station in one of my least favoured areas. I stepped back from the presiding officer as two Rastas came in to vote. The smallest voted and left, but the larger guy, having voted, turned and wished my luck. Stepping outside the hut, Sally was sitting in the car and lighting the smaller Rasta's cigarette, when the big guy said hey, don't you realise you've just voted for Mr Brandon-Bravo ! It was only two votes, but who would have expected they would be for a Conservative. Some time later we realised, that they must have been friends of the meter winder, and knew I wasn't such a bad guy after all.

If you're a good boy you get to go on a few really good freebies ! In fairness these are essential if a member is to have a broad understanding of both Home and Foreign Affairs. I was privileged to join a defence group down to the Falklands in 1984, where the Labour Member for Coventry laid a wreath over the sunken wreck of that destroyer, and our group leader Carol Mather, who had been a colonel in the Welsh Guards which had fought valiantly there during the war, also went to pay respects to those who had fallen. The Ghurkhas were in resident at the time, various regiments having six months tours of duty there, and they held a small reception for us. Whilst chatting away, I was offered a drink and asked for a scotch. Whilst my back was turned a scotch, and I mean a large scotch, had been poured, and I had to keep a straight face as I consumed it. They are great little people, but watch out when they pour the drinks !

On West Falklands we met a farmer who looked after some 32000 acres with just 32000 sheep grazing. That was a measure of just how poor the land is, but it was a living for him and his family, wife, daughter and one farmhand. His hobby was as a radio ham, which came in very handy during the war. He had a tall triangular metal radio mast, which came into use as soon as he spotted Argie planes coming over West Falklands when our troops were landing and defending Falkland Sound. His message went via Ascension Island to the War Cabinet, and back down to the Sound, giving our troops a few moments to prepare for the attack. He could not understand why the Argies just flew over his farm, without seeking to take out the mast. He had only been to Stanley a few times, and his daughter had only been to Stanley once, but she didn't like it, it was too noisy ! Stanley at that time had just over 600 residents, and the only hotel was the famous Upland Goose, and I wonder what her reaction would be if she came for a visit to London.

I had two other defence department trips to Belize, and saw the excellent job performed by our troops there, and the unique training facilities Belize afforded. Their one big problem was the climate, for it had the unique ability to rot through the steelwork of military vehicles in incredibly short order. It's a tiny multicultural country, where all groups seem to live happily together, and indeed there were five different ethnic groups represented in the six parliamentarians who entertained us out on the quays. The troop's R and R was out on the quays and we were taken out in one of those helicopters like a fly's eye where you can look down between your feet and scan the shallows below. The sergeant in charge, asked that I didn't report back, since he had been there many tours longer than expected, and that it was the best posting he'd ever had, and he hoped he had been forgotten. Burnt brown as a berry, and clearly as fit as a fiddle, I could see why he wanted to keep his head down. There was a road to the Guatemalan border, and manned by a British guard force. From the opposite side a road had been built right up to the border, on the basis that given the Guatemalan claim on Belize, it would one day allow them to complete the road to the Atlantic coast. We did go across the border, for on our side was a map of central America showing Belize and Guatemala, but from the other side the map showed no Belize and Guatemala stretching from the Pacific to the Atlantic coasts.

We flew by chopper to the south of the country where the landing pad was so small, that they dare not turn off the engine whilst we disembarqued, in case for whatever reason they might be unable to restart the engines. They flew off, and rejoined us some hour or so later. The site overlooked the river that was the only outlet to the Atlantic from Guatemala, and hence of strategic interest to both countries. We flew on to a settlement in the jungle where a community of very small – not exactly pigmies – lived, and the excitement particularly of the children, was quite heart warming. We brought the gift of some footballs, and we could not have chosen better.

The second visit had an amusing twist. There is a long, straight, narrow road leading from Belize City to the north, and we noticed that at regular intervals there were stout steel poles driven into the ground. It transpired that these were to try to deter the small planes that transported drugs from South America to the USA from landing and being refuelled on deserted stretches of the road. One of the successful drug seizures by the Belize police, resulted in a top of the range limo being confiscated and handed to the Vice President for his official duties. He paid a price for his home was burnt down a few weeks later. But this was further compounded, for when the car was taken in for service, they found drugs stuffed into whatever space there was behind panels. Apart from the embarrassment, we were told later that he took it all in good part.

An exchange visit to the US Congress and Senate followed a visit by a Senator to England, who came to see live, Prime Minster's question time. As he stood on the floor of the Chamber, he remarked as to how small it was, but more important he said "If we had the equivalent of Prime Minister's question time for our Presidents, we would have very different Presidents". After a thought he added, "Come to think of it, we would have very different Senators!" That trip to the States took me to a congressman in Florida, and I joined him at one of his fund raisers in a Wild West theme bar. Having made his pitch, he announced that with him was a guy from the mother of Parliaments, and I had to climb up to the balcony and quickly find something to say. After very brief pleasantries, I told them I'd just been re-elected and that my maximum spend would have been no more than 12000 dollars. There was a hoot of laughter, and someone shouted that it would not buy 10 seconds of TV time. Another quickly shouted, "What a great idea!".

Late in 1988, shortly after the Palestine Liberation

Organisation had convened their Parliament, and had indicated they were at last considering recognising the State of Israel in order that talks towards a settlement might take place, the Inter parliamentary Union accepted an invitation from the Tunisian Government, to send a small delegation on a planned interchange of members between our two countries. Although the trip was primarily to discuss their past and planned constitutional structure, their aim to facilitate an honourable settlement of the Israel/Palestine problem was top of their agenda. Through our ambassador Stephen Day, three of us Ted Ledbitter, Eddy Loyden and I agreed to meet PLO representatives, providing they understood that I was Jewish and a member of the Conservative Friends of Israel, and that Ted was similarly a member of Labour's friends of Israel.

We met in a safe house with the PLO "Foreign Secretary" Farouk Kadoumi, who was also secretary of the Fatah organisation, Dr Zehdi Terzi their UN delegate, and Abu Jaffar the director of their political department. The meeting lasted for two hours and with our ambassador and Mr Simon Collis taking notes, and we made it clear we were there simply to listen. Kadoumi took us at our word, and we were given a lecture lasting three quarters of an hour, interrupted only in mid flow by his indicating that he knew I was the Jew. He made clear that whatever the wording of their "Parliamentary" declaration confirming recognition of the State of Israel, he would have none of it, and that it would not succeed. He made clear that even if a two State solution was agreed, it would not last and that his ultimate aim was a single Palestinian State, and that all Palestinians should be repatriated and returned to the homes they occupied prior to the War of 1948. Given we were there to listen, not to negotiate, I did not try to point out the much greater number of Jewish people were ejected from their homes throughout North Africa and the Middle East, and therefore forced willingly or otherwise to settle in Israel. In the discussion that followed, Dr Terzi underlined the fact that the Arab world was at war with Israel, yet failed to recognise that alone made it almost impossible for Israel to negotiate with people who refused to recognise them or to accept their right to exist. Both made it clear that any recognition of the State of Israel could only come after negotiations were complete, for they could not recognise it as a lawful state until boundaries were agreed, yet that was precisely what they were asking the world to do in respect of a Palestinian State. Frankly I came away from that meeting feeling that nothing had changed, and that the recent declaration was little more than a PR exercise designed to bolster support for their cause in the wider world.

In our home village of Barton in Fabis, we had some Greek Cypriot friends, and inevitably I took an interest in the troubles of that Island. I'd been to stay with these friends at their home which they had retained in Cyprus, and visited the home of his family whose house was close to the Green Line dividing the North from the South. What struck me sitting in their garden was that you could see barely 200 yards away, a line of flags marking the so called boundary. The vast majority of the flags were those of Greece, and were interspersed with the odd flag of Cyprus itself. On the other side they were faced with a few flags that were of Turkey. On meeting one of their Parliamentarians I could not help but point out, that if the National Flags of Greece and Turkey were the major display, how on earth were they ever to resolve their problems. Part of the stand off was economic, for the North supplied the water, and the South the electricity, something that no doubt has been resolved by now.

Inevitably I wanted to see the problem from the other side, and in April of 1989 had the chance to visit Northern Cyprus. This did cause some difficulty with some of our friend's colleagues in their local community, but in the end they did accept that if MPs were ever going to be able to assist in any way to resolve the problems in the island, then we had to have seen the arguments from both sides. Sir Fergus Montgomery led our little group of six, which included two Northern Island

Meeting Australian PM Bob Hawke with a delegation led by Alf Morris in 1990

members, Cecil Walker and Roy Beggs. We had to touch down first in Turkey, not even stopping over, for no direct flights were allowed, as such flights would be deemed to be recognising the State of Northern Cyprus. Therefore only flights coming in from Turkey were allowed. We had most informative meeting with Rauf Denktash, and senior members of his government, four of whom were educated in England. Mr Denktash had spent a lot of time in Liverpool, their Speaker Mr Hakki Atun, had been educated in Nottingham, and their representative in London Tansel Fikri in Sheffield. We met many who had fled north after 1974, losing everything, and were now subject to the discussions on swop arrangements with Greek Cypriots who had fled South, likewise leaving their land and properties behind. One of the many civilians we met was a Mr John Kent, a British citizen of Turkish origin, married to a Scottish wife and whose children had been educated in the UK. Mr Kent had tried to correspond with our Foreign Office to be told that unless return mail was addressed to Turkey, it would not be delivered to Northern Cyprus. His MP back home was Ivor Stanbrook, was bringing such difficulties to the attention of Ministers. I asked Mr Denktash whether he foresaw a time when his community in Northern Cyprus would be seen as inconvenient to Turkey. He felt that whoever governed Turkey would not survive what he felt sure would be seen as a desertion of their own. Thirty years on the problem is still there.

My most fascinating trip was to the Yemen on a human rights mission, for we understood that whilst most Yemeni Jews had long left to settle in Israel, there were perhaps a thousand still there in villages north of Sanaa. That exodus was quite extraordinary, for the Jewish community in the Yemen had been there for a few thousand years, and was perhaps one of the oldest in the world. Apparently in 1948 or 9 the Israelis sent some old DC10s to try to bring them to Israel. The fear was that such a primitive group would simply not board the plane. However they gathered their goats and belongings, and without fear boarded the plane, but had to be restrained from lighting cooking fires. It transpired that the "good book" had always said that one day they would return to the Promised Land on wings of eagles. For them the DC10s were just that. We had a most friendly and informative meeting with the Yemini foreign minister, Dr Abul Karim Al-Eryani, who expressed sorrow at what might be the loss of the remaining tiny Jewish community, who he referred to as Jewish Yemenis rather than Yemeni Jews, a subtle difference that was not lost on us. He spoke of the possible loss of the remaining Jewish community as a loss of 4000 years of civilisation. Accompanied by our ambassador we had a narrow escape when his heavily armoured land-rover slid over the edge on a rough road, and thankfully came to rest on a ledge that stopped before what we feared would be a tumble down into a deep gorge.

Some 100 miles north of Sanaa, we met the local Sheik who entertained us and arranged for us to visit his Jews. As ever, Greville Janner who as a member of the magic circle, could always break the ice with his tricks, and having scored a great success with the young son of the sheik, our attendance at the Sheik's weekly feast with guests was quite something. It was a long carpet spread the length of the room, and we and other visitors sat on the floor along its length whilst food was piled on the carpet. Greville found himself as the favoured guest and sitting opposite the Sheik, whilst I, thank goodness, was well down the carpet. I was happy to eat the honey and slices of sorghum in front of me, but poor Greville had all sorts of heaven knows what fed to him by the Sheik. I'm sure it wasn't kosher, but we were in the Sheik's territory! We met one of the three Jewish families still living in the village, and apart from their ringlets, and the absence of any guns or knives, they were to all intents and purposes, Yemenis. Greville and I agreed to join them for their Friday night supper, and to stay for their customary evening service. Whilst they were anxious to offer traditional hospitality, we were conscious of their poverty and the inevitable simple fare provided, and so we endeavoured to take the smallest possible portions of their food without risking offence. A very old and almost blind elder, started the service, but promptly handed over to a young boy, who I don't think was yet old enough to have been barmitvah. I found myself listening to a service I could have attended as a small boy pre-war in the Stoke Newington Synagogue, for it was the same, unchanged service for a couple of thousand years. The boy also had problems with his eyes, and Greville managed to arrange for him to come to England for an operation, which I believe was funded by an American ex-Yemeni citizen, who had helping to sustain the small remaining community in the Yemen.

We were accompanied by a truck with a mounted machine gun and crew, to another village where we were to meet another Jewish family. We stopped to seek directions from someone in the local market, who readily showed us where Sala the Jew lived. It was a Saturday, and arriving at his house, it was closed up and the large steel doors closed. Greville banged on the steel doors, and a face appeared framed in a small upper window. It for all intents and purposes it was Shylock from the Merchant of Venice! Shouting it was Shabbat, and go away, Greville finally managed to get him to understand we were Jewish and wished to pay our respects. We were let in and joined Sala and the rest of the male members of the family, in the customary post lunch chewing of quat. As ever in that part of the world, the women were not to be seen.

A short visit to the local market was instructive, for it naturally divided into separate lanes dependant on what was for sale. One lane sold little else but salt. Another farm produce, and another had a row of large containers, who's front doors were open to display every kind of gun, AK47s, RPGs, you could wish for, and we managed to photograph a few of our party, capturing one of the containers in the background.

I had the opportunity to act as an observer in October 1988 at the plebiscite in Chile, called by Pinochet to decide whether he should serve another term on a straight forward Yes or No question. A colleague Jacques Arnold and I were sent there by the Inter-Parliamentary Union, and were joined by Dawn Primarola and George Foulkes from the Labour Party, along with journalists, some of whom were so convinced that it was either a stitch up, or that Pinochet would not accept the result if it went against him, that they had already drafted most of their reports. In addition to the delegation from the UK, observers from twenty nine other countries were welcomed by the Apainde group (Parliamentary Association for Democracy).

Before leaving we were briefed by Mr Patrick Morgan of our South American Department, and by the Chilean Ambassador Senor Juan Carlos Delanu. We were met on arrival by Mr Jack Thompson from our embassy, and shown round central Santiago. We climbed Mount Santa Lucia, a popular recreation area where dozen of young people were doing what young people world wide will do in a public park in glorious sunshine ! It seemed a million miles away from what was to be a momentous and vital election.

Not something we're used to in campaign procedure in the UK, but the Saturday prior to polling day, was set aside for the NO rallies and their campaign finale, and the Sunday for the SI. During these last two days of campaigning the boulevards in the city were crowded with decorated cars and floats, creating quite a carnival atmosphere. Election literature was hurled around like a New York ticker tape reception, so that at the conclusion of campaigning it could be said that you literally were walking ankle deep in paperwork. These were followed by two days where campaigning was banned, and people were left with time for quiet reflection on which way to vote.

One note of amusement arose from the recognition that there was one kind of "honking" if you were a NO supporter, and another if you supported the SI campaign. Cowards that we were, our car horn answered favourably to whichever "honk" we received. However when having answered favourably to a NO "honk", a young person looked carefully into our car and made it plain that he recognised a bunch of middle class hypocrites. That Sunday, Patrick Morgan took us to the home of a recently returned Chilean Embassy official from London, Sr. Manuel Cardenas. We travelled on the Metro to a very pleasant outer suburb, and could not help but remark on the superb quality of the Metro system, and above all the spotless nature of the stations and trains, to a standard we could only dream of back home.

We used the two day pause to see a bit of the country, and drove up into the foothills of the Andes accompanied by Manuel and Maricruz Cadenas and Patrick Morgan. We stopped for refreshment at a wayside café, and found that the very elderly owner had a lifetime ambition to see London. His daughter brought out his treasured collection of photographs of London scenes, but we didn't have the heart to tell him that the London of today was a very different scene to the Victorian London portrayed in his album.

We split up on polling day, and I was accompanied by Mr and

Mrs Peter Holmes from our embassy to two towns, firstly to Buin some thirty miles from Santiago, and then to Rancagua ninety miles from the capital. We arrived at an all women station, and as we walked towards the polling booth, my guides heard one of the women in a derogatory way refer to us as Americans. No No Peter Holmes said, we are from England and this is a British MP. At this they immediately cried "Mrs Thatcher", and burst into applause. Being nowhere from nowhere, the impact Mrs T had around the world could not have been better demonstrated.

The method of voting seemed much more secure and confidential than our own, for firstly women voted not just in separate polling booths, but in separate polling stations, avoiding male pressure that does affect some of our own elections. The ballot papers gave greater confidentiality, for the number on the ballot paper was removed before being handed to the voter, and the ballot box had a clear Perspex panel so that it was clear the vote had been cast and correctly boxed.

We gathered in the hotel awaiting the results, and as they came in, it was clear the answer would be No, but it was also clear that whilst the women had also voted No, they were far less anti Pinochet than the men. The journalists waited until Pinochet had publicly accepted the verdict of the people before they tore up their scripts and started again. Amongst the impressions and memories I brought back, was firstly that whatever its limitations, the outcome was clearly the wish of the Chilean people. Secondly and sadly, a distaste for those journalists representing newspapers of repute, some politicians who ought to know better, and some British students barely out of their nappies who perhaps could therefore be forgiven, who came to Chile with their slogans, prejudices, and pre-written articles announcing fraud, which of course turned out to be anything but the truth.

Jacques had been born in Brazil, and had spent much of his commercial life dealing in finance throughout South America, and called on a few old friends. I could not believe how many secure cash trucks raced from Bank to Bank, many of which had been founded by British immigrants some 100 years earlier, and I soon could spot the "suits" with their secure briefcases, also hawking cash from place to place. Jacques fancied a meal in what he called the Meats restaurant, and ordered a large steak. I wasn't particularly hungry and agreed to have something small and light and ordered a couple of kidneys. When they arrived, I swear they must have slaughtered an elephant, for I'd never seen kidneys the size of dinner plates before. Needless to say I had an uncomfortable 24 hours before my metabolism returned to normal.

Twice during my time in the House, I was able to act as an election observer in two elections in Bangladesh in 1986 and 91. The former had been called by General Ershad, who was seeking electoral backing for his continued Presidency. Our small delegation was lead by Lord Ennals at the invitation of the People's Commission for Free Elections, effectively their equivalence of our Law Society and Judges, and their embassy in London gave us clearance to attend. Following our arrival we received a warm welcome from leading members of some of the Parties, Awami League, Jamaat-eIslami, Jatio Samajtantrik Dal, the Bangladesh Nationalist Party and the Bangladesh Khilafat Movement. Only the Jatiya Party were not prepared to meet us.

David Ennals, a long standing friend of Bangladesh, was obviously sympathetic to the cause of the Awami League, but we agreed that we should not take sides or seek to pass opinions, but simply record what we saw at polling stations, and let the figures speak for themselves.

The ballot papers were wondrous to behold, for they displayed a large emblem of each Party, and because of the many Parties, often had to be eighteen inches long. The books of ballot papers were not perforated so that when illegally fistfuls of papers were torn out for ballot box stuffing, it was easy to see what had happened, and that the normal issue of one paper at a time had been ignored. Each Polling Station inside had rows of seats, or rather wooden planks, so that representatives of the parties could see that the process was fair and correct. It was totally ineffective in most of the stations we visited, and some of the conduct was, to put it mildly, violent. Certainly by the afternoon certain elements had clearly swung into action to frustrate free and fair elections.

I was accompanied by a barrister, and at a station around midday, the presiding officer proudly showed me his register. He claimed that only two more people were to be expected, and he would then have a 100% turnout ! I checked the register, and apart from some dubious names that my barrister noted, it was dated May 1983. I asked my interpreter to complement the presiding officer on what must have been the outstanding quality of the local health service. When this was duly passed on, to the puzzlement of my guide and the officer, I pointed out that the register was three years old, and so not one person in that small town had died ! At another I was greeted by a small boy whose hands were covered with the purple dye that was supposed to be on the one finger that had been used to vote, by pressing against the symbol of the party of his choice. He claimed to have voted many times, and looking at his hands, I had little doubt that he had.

At another, the presiding officer had locked himself in his office, because not being Bengali, was being accused of favouring some voters against others. At another, a woman was brought in on a small cart, for she had been attacked and had a gash from her hip to her knee. My last station was at the University in Dacca, and being after six o'clock, I duly noted the total electorate, and the number of votes cast at that time. My feeling was that if the returns suddenly showed a full turnout, the credibility of the election would rightly be called into question. As we were leaving the station, we were greeted by gunfire in the road outside, caused by a large group who had already trashed a polling station some mile further back. I quietly asked my guide where our Land-Rover was, and having noted the distance, said –"let's get the hell out of here". On returning to the hotel, we were greeted by a hilarious group of journalists who had just left a meeting called by General Ershad. He had stopped the election count, for it wasn't coming out the way he had planned, and when journalists spoke of the malpractices at the polling stations, he complained about our delegation, though we had said nothing at that point. In any case he claimed that there had only been malpractice reported at 268 polling stations. He could not see the funny side of his remarks. We had a wash-up meeting with our hosts, and when asked, I had sadly to say their election was almost irrelevant to the majority of Bangladeshis, since we had been told that the population was growing at around two and a half million a year, that the country could no longer feed its people, and relied on 86% of its income from overseas aid. I said I felt that until they resolved that conundrum, it was unlikely any Government could obtain the willing support of its people or solve it's problems.

When I returned from that first election I bumped into Norman Tebbitt who was our Party Chairman at that time, and remarked that if he wanted to win the next election with a big majority, "have I found a system for you"! Whilst the second election was a much better run affair, the population had grown even faster than had first been calculated, and therefore the country's problems were as intractable as ever.

The second election there in February 1991 was led by Peter Shore with Andrew Bennett from the Labour Party, and David Wilshire and I from the Conservatives. On this occasion the group had been formally invited by the Acting President Shahabuddin, with the Election Commission chaired by the Chief Justice Rouf. The atmosphere of this second election was totally different from the first, for all the stations we visited were calm, and people were seen voting without fear of interference from either police or army personnel. There were of course minor examples of malpractice spotted, but most were stopped by presiding officers who on this occasion seemed confident to act without fear of reprisal. There was the odd case where young boys tried to vote, but were turned away with little more than an indulgent smile. The one truly bad case was an electoral role that had no more than a few percentage of names of genuine voters, and rafts of names that were clearly fictitious. Visiting polling stations both in the City of Dacca, and in the Sylhet region gave us a real picture of what we felt was a reasonably free and fair election.

On arrival at the Dacca Airport to return home, we checked in our bags and proceeded as we thought to board the plane. We found ourselves at yet another counter where staff were chalk marking cases that they approved for loading, and heard a German traveller having a fearful row with one of the staff who was demanding money before he would pass through his bags. I think it was David who said it was not worth making a fuss, so we paid up and got all our kit stowed onboard.

I was picked to join a delegation led by Gwyneth Dunwoody to Botswana and Swaziland to run a seminar on local and central government. Botswana seemed a settled country whose population was almost exclusively of the Swana tribe, and perhaps highlighted why some African countries which had been put together by European settlers, and which had two or more distinct tribes, have had such trouble coming to terms with their national identity.

In a break we flew to the nature reserve in the north of the country, and were met on the rough landing strip by a choir from a local school. The children sang a lovely little song of welcome, written by their school mistress, and when Gwyneth stepped up to reply, she sang her response to the same tune. I was amazed at such a talent, and said so, only to be even more surprised to be told that as a youngster she had been a singer and had trod the boards. We struck up a friendship, and we agreed to pair by arrangement with the whips office, once we were back in Westminster.

The Swaziland seminar was attended by one of the country's princesses, a very large and jovial lady, who listened attentively to our presentations. She retired with Gwyneth to a side room, but one of her attendants came out and asked that I join them for further discussions, since the princess preferred my slant on politics to Gwyneth's. As so often in Parliament, you can fundamentally disagree with a member of an opposing Party, and still be friends. One of our hosts was a South African Brit, who had lived there all of his life, and had fought in the South African Rifles during WW11. On returning to Swaziland he had been appointed to the King's Government and had retired a few years later. His wife was very talented and on their retirement had established a new business producing fabrics using natural dyes. They lived in a hilltop home which we all christened Sangri La, such was the beauty of the spot. We stood in his garden and he pointed out in the distant far north, the faint outline of a mountain. He then pointed south to a similar mountain. You know, he said, some idiot in the Foreign Office early in the 20th Century, drew a line between the two mountains and the following morning a third of the Swazi tribe found themselves living outside Swaziland in a different country. Looking at the straight lines on many African countries, one can see we have much to answer for.

For some years, Sally and I had joined the campaign to allow Russian Jews to be allowed to leave Russia. I had been surprised to hear from the Jubilee Committee, which made a presentation to MPs at Westminster, that neither of our Church Leaders in either the Cof E, or the Catholic Church, had sought to help Christian refusniks, presumably on the grounds that they did not want to make waves, and cause even greater trouble for Christians in Russia. As a result the Jubilee Committee had taken up the challenge, and I and many others agreed to assist, pointing out that members of the Jewish community had been running such a campaign for years. Our first success was a nun who was released and went to live in West Germany. However she was released as a dissenting Jew, and added to the quota of Jewish refusnics granted leave to emigrate, so that there was no record of any persecution of Christians in Russia.

A human rights visit to Eastern Europe, gave us the unique opportunity to be in Berlin as the Wall came down, and to visit what for a while longer was still the DDR. The trip took us to Czechoslovakia, and to Prague where our resident ambassador could barely bring himself to give us a cup of tea. The day of arrival coincided with their currency being halved in value to the pound, so we did very well indeed. Going out for supper in a hotel overlooking the river in Prague, we noticed the customary display cabinet in the reception area, and we promptly relieved them of its entire offering of beautiful cut glass wear. We naturally visited the concentration camp of Terezenstadt (Terezin) which was supposed to have been the better face of that outrage to humanity. Looking at the ovens - it wasn't supposed to be an extermination camp – the taps over the sinks that were not connected to anything, and the wooden shelves that supposedly served as beds, made you think that the International Red Cross were either deaf, blind and dumb, or they were complicit in the evil that was being perpetrated there. One of our party was Lynn Golding the Labour member for Stoke on Trent, who made one of the most moving and influential speeches in the House, during the third reading of the War Crimes Bill. We entrained briefly to Budapest, and I had the chance to meet up with my old friend and rowing colleague Jonny Szabo the Israeli Rowing President, who still tried to spend a couple of months each year in the land of his birth, but would never consider a permanent return.

Our journey home was broken with a two day stopover in Vienna where we had a chance to spend an hour or so at the Plaza Hotel with Simon Weisenthal. He came over as a kind and gentle character, but the underlying steel and determination that had driven him all those years was also very apparent.

Sally and I joined a human rights group visiting Russian

refusniks in October 91, to what just three weeks before had become St Petersburg. Our aim was to assist those still locked in the no mans land between perestroika and the state bureaucracy fighting to maintain its reason for being. We met a family living in a flat in an old pre-revolution building where three or more families shared certain facilities. They had two rooms and a kitchen which doubled as a bathroom, with a large wooden board to cover the bath when not in use. The two rooms had to double as both living and bedrooms. It had been the home for the couple and their two grown up children. At one stage, they also had to make room for the wife of one of the sons, until they were allocated a home of their own. The parents had applied to be allowed to emigrate seven years before, but because the man had worked in computers, it was presumed he was aware of Government IT secrets, and hence was not allowed to emigrate. In addition to the "State Secrets" excuse, the addition of the "poor relation" clearance requirement was an equal block to a hoped for emigration visa. When we returned we wrote the usual letters to the Russian Embassy and were pleased that after a few months they were granted the right to leave, and they settled in California working for IBM.

Our Hotel was on the main square with the "Leningrad" parliament building at one end, and a magnificent church at the other. It was owned by a Finnish company who were banking on the opening up of the Russian economy allowing them to at least take some of their profits home. A Scottish baker had opened a business there, but because he could not transfer money back home, he could not buy the things he needed to build his business, and it had folded very quickly. We did have a laugh at one of our group's expense, for at our first meal, what we may have ordered came in fits and starts, and we agreed to accept whatever was placed in front of us. Baroness Nancy Seer was a lovely lady, but when confronted with her "pudding" remarked that someone has stolen my cherry ! When the remark sank in, she joined in the general hilarity.

The economics of the new Russia were beyond understanding. Our hotel operated on the basis that all charges were based on an exchange rate of two roubles to the dollar, but the official rate was 200 to the dollar. Out on the main street, the Nevsky Prospekt, you could get 800 roubles to the dollar. We took some Jewish students out for a meal in a pub/restaurant that only took hard currency, and when a student looked at the cost of the dishes on offer, he remarked that he could have had a weeks holiday on the Black Sea for the price of the meal. Six months later I related this tale to the Ukrainian Club in my constituency, when someone in the audience called out that the rate was now 2000 roubles to the dollar. One student asked when Sally and I were going to emigrate to Israel. We asked why would we since we were British citizens, and my family had roots going back over 300 years in England. He was puzzled and asked what was in our passports, and when we replied, why British of course, he pointed out that in Russia if you were Jewish, then that would be in your passport.

We discovered, though not surprised, that along with perestroika came a rise in anti-Semitism. The same old hate literature such as the Protocols of The Elders of Zion, could be bought on the streets, but there had been great gains as well. After years of being locked and sealed, the Institute of Oriental Studies could now show us the treasures of old Hebrew manuscripts, and the recently reopened synagogue overflowed with thousands seeking to attend High Holy Day services. One of the elders however explained that there were now three categories of Soviet Jews – those who have left – those planning to leave – and those who hope they won't have to go.

When we returned, Douglas Hogg asked if I would come and see him for a full debrief of our visit. He had held responsibility for Russian affairs for perhaps nine months at that point, and queried this information with his senior civil servant present. With a Sir Humphrey like pause, the civil servant confirmed our story, and the look on Douglas's face said it all.

This was not the only example of Civil Servants holding information back from Ministers, or passing on only what they thought was appropriate. After the 1987 election, Cyril Smith wrote to Douglas highlighting his belief that there had been wide examples of personation in a few of his wards in his Rochdale constituency. Knowing I had a large ethnic population in my constituency, Douglas asked me to join him at a meeting with Cyril. Cyril outlined the pattern of turnout in his constituency, highlighting a much higher turnout in certain wards, that could only have been achieved if personation had taken place. Since I had had a number of such cases, I felt it would be right for Douglas to order some research by his officers. A few weeks later, he sent me the draft of the letter he planned to send to Cyril, but I stopped him in time. His officers had come up with a tiny figure of less than one percent nationally, and therefore there was no case for any major concern or action. I pointed out that since vast areas of the country had few if any of certain minorities, I was not surprised that statistically on a National level there wasn't a problem, but it justified Cyril's claim of 15% personation in some of his wards. You will make your own judgment as to whether those who did the research and drafted Douglas' letter were either grossly inefficient, ignorant, or deliberately fudging the issue. However as a result, in the 1992 election, many polling stations, where deemed necessary, displayed notices making clear that such actions were unlawful.

My most interesting overseas Parliamentary trips were to Israel, where Sally and I had been twice before in 1964 and 67. One group in 1986, led by Peter Thomas the past Secretary of State for Wales, were sent as a prelude to Shimon Peres their prime Minister coming to the UK, and Mrs T making an official visit to Israel. The group included Dr John Blackburn, Michael Brown, Edward Leigh and Anna McCurley. Ministers are naturally accustomed to meeting senior ministers of other countries in the course of their duties, so I and I'm sure the other backbenchers felt privileged to meet all the principle ministers, and leaders of the opposition, and hearing first hand particularly of the problems thrown up by their proportional electoral system. I felt confirmed in the view that whatever the short comings of our first past the post system, it at least produced a government that felt able to act without being stymied by numerous tiny minority parties. The Speaker Mr Shlomo Hillel was very open about these problems, and pointed out that twenty seven different groups had fought the previous election and fifteen of these won representation in the Knesset. That is why it has for so long been almost impossible for a single Party to have the mandate and Parliamentary muscle to resolve the Palestinian/Israel issue which clearly the majority of Israelis pray for. What also became very clear, no tiny minority Party was going to agree to a change in the electoral system if the result would be their extinction.

Our discussions with Abba Eban clearly underlined and confirmed the esteem in which he was widely held in international circles. However some years later to the surprise of many outside Israel, Abba Eban disappeared from the scene, a victim of the absurd list system that allows Parties to list their candidates in order of the Party's preference, not the voting

The tobacco lobby on its fruitless annual visit to the Chancellor

public's, and being low down on his party's list, he failed to be re-elected. Shimon Peres who came across as clearly a man genuinely seeking a fair and peaceful solution to a settlement with the Palestinians. However the government was a coalition, and he was shortly handing over the top role to Yitzhak Shamir who was less enamoured with the deal Israel had made with Egypt, and simply commented that they had given us peace, and we gave them Sinai !

We toured the borders of the country, but the most impressive visit was to Massada, which prompted Peter Thomas to remark that he'd been to many places in the world, but none had moved him quite as much as Massada. Although the Dead Sea had shrunk a long way from the base of the redoubt, the slope the Romans had built to enable them to finally take the site could still be seen, and the water cisterns built into the rock were still there to demonstrate how the community had been able to survive for as long as they did.

In 1990 Alf Morris lead a team of five to Australia to return to them the Charter of their Federation in 1901, and it gave me a chance to meet for the first time, family members who had settled in Australia after the first World War. My father was one of twelve siblings, and five of his brothers had emigrated to Australia in 1922/3, three to Sydney and two to Melbourne. My cousin, known as Berry, had been born on the ship the Berryman before they landed down under, and was named after the ship. He became a taxi driver, and later ran a retirement home. He was the split-image of my father, so it was without difficulty I recognised him when he came to our hotel on the Friday evening of our arrival. With Alf's consent, I left my colleagues to join Berry and the family for their Friday night supper. I had corresponded with Berry ever since I became involved in local and then national government, and was staggered and delighted when on arriving at his home I found welcoming signs surrounded with all my past election literature. Entering the house, I was even more delighted to find around fourteen or more members of my extended family gathering for a traditional Jewish Friday night supper. To say the red carpet had been rolled out would be a master of understatement, and the scene was that which would have been replicated around the world by Jewish families for whom the eve of Sabbath was something special and to be treasured. Much as I enjoyed meeting the Prime Minister Bob Hawke, the Speaker, and many other distinguished Parliamentarians, it was that family gathering that remains my overriding memory of that trip. With Rowing being my great interest outside politics, our trip to Canberra gave me the opportunity to see how the creation of an Institute for Sport could make an impact for good both on raising standards, and encouraging participation. I brought back copious papers and information on the set-up and handed them to Robert Atkins, the then Minister of Sport. Sadly nothing appeared to happen until after 1992 when John Major proposed the creation of a similar Institute for England. One of the Australian Parliamentarians came to the UK on the return visit, just at the time of Mrs Thatchers final speech to the House, following her decision not to stand in the second round of voting for the leadership. He and his colleagues sat in the gallery to hear that speech, and when we met up afterwards, his profuse admiration for Mrs T's speech was such that I could not help but agree with the sentiment "What on earth have we done!"

With peace having been established between Israel and Egypt in 1977, a great step forward for peace in the Middle East, it sadly resulted in the assassination of Egypt's President Anwar Sadat, by those for whom peace was not, and is not, an option, Sally and I planned a holiday in Egypt. A friend – not a constituent - who had family in Egypt and Jordan insisted that if we were going there, his family would be offended if we did not allow them to offer us some hospitality. We also met up with old friends from the World of Rowing and spent a couple of days with an International Umpire Fayaz Yakan and his wife. They lived in a small block of ten flats, where the tenants had collectively agreed to look after the building for their own quality and standard of living. It appeared then, that once a rent was agreed, that was it forever, and understandably properties simply were never maintained by their owners. We suffered in the UK for that approach to housing for far too long after WW11.

We had obtained diplomatic passport stamps and duly had a wonderful week in Egypt and then flew to Amman to join the rest of his family. The head of the family ran one of the largest shipping and transport companies in the Middle East, but it turned out that they were either born in Palestine, or were the sons and daughters of the old matriarch who left there in 1948. He remembered sitting on guard as a local Palestinian, employed by the British Authorities, in a small pillbox down on the Red Sea, at what is now the great resort of Elat. One of the company directors who helped us to tour around, pointed out that he was the only true Jordanian in the business; the family many still technically Palestinian. This was highlighted when he pointed out that historically the West had bequeathed King Abdulla land rather than a Kingdom, for pre-48 the town of Amman had probably no more than 60,000 inhabitants, and with a total population of Jordan no more than 100,000. Now that Amman had 1.2 million, and the total population of 3.2 million, the majority were clearly of Palestinian origin. Those who had settled post 1948 but prior to 1967 were given full Jordanian citizenship, but those who came later only have laissez passé documents and are not citizens. Sadly the granting of citizenship is not common throughout Middle Eastern countries, leaving families of two or more generations, settled for sixty years or more still being treated as refugees, and so keeping the Palestinian/Israeli issue as a running sore.

On arrival at the airport in Amman I presented what turned out to be a newly issued passport for me, but Sally still had an old one with an Israeli stamp in it. At passport control they commented politely but firmly that she had been to the enemy, and I said I'd been there too, but they were happy since my passport did not have the unacceptable Israeli stamp in it. However they were most helpful, and on signing a piece of paper guaranteeing that we would go to the embassy and get a fresh passport for Sally, and bring it back to the airport, they would stamp it and grant access. On arrival at the embassy the ambassador, Mr Tony Reeve, came to see us and told us not to worry and he sent a driver back to the airport to get the new passport stamped. He then invited us to join them that evening at a reception for the Anglo Jordanian Association and a buffet supper.

It gave us the chance to meet a number of current and retired ministers of the Jordanian Government, including a few sitting members of their Parliament including two holding seats from Nablus and Jennin on the West Bank. They were currently discussing the form and timing of a new Parliament, the Maglis, for just the East Bank which we now recognise as Jordan, without members from the West Bank who then had seats in the Jordanian Maglis. It did highlight the view held by some, that since "Transjordan" had covered both sides of the River Jordan, what was the legitimacy of the Palestinian State. I agree that time has moved on, and the rights of Palestinians to have a country of their own are beyond dispute, but you cannot totally ignore the historical background to many of these issues. However there was a clear conviction expressed that the UK could and should play a unique role as a friend and catalyst in the search for peace. Back home, with time to ponder on what we had seen and heard, I came to the sad conclusion, that notwithstanding the clear desire of so many to find an honourable and peaceful solution to the Israel/Palestine issue, there were just too many that would object to a Jordanian/Israel peace, and certainly a peace between Israel and the Palestinians. Within months, the first intifada – rebellion – broke out in December 1987, highlighting my worst fears.

When the first gulf war broke out in 1991, four back benchers were sent to Israel to underpin the view of the Government and

Opposition, that Israel, unless extremely provoked, should avoid being drawn in, and thereby split the Arab world that supported our campaign to throw Saddam out of Kuwait. It was a most ecumenical foursome of two Jews, one Ashkenazi and one Sephardi, two Christians, one Catholic and one Protestant. The team were Stuart Bell, Michael Brown, Greville Janner and me. The scuds were falling on Israel, though whilst causing considerable damage, thankfully only killed four people. There was also the fear of gas, and everyone carried a gas mask. When they were issued to us, I showed my age by being the only one who had tried similar masks as a youngster before WW11. Their ministers were well aware of the risks should they be so provoked, and fortunately they held their hand, and the war was brought to a satisfactory conclusion. Only later did the feeling grow, that perhaps a further 24 hours, might have seen Saddam so weakened that the second gulf war might well have been avoided.

Not all of these "freebees" were overseas, and one of my most fascinating defence trips was to the submarine base in Scotland, and a trip on one of our giant Conqueror class nuclear submarines. We entered deep water and were asked if one of us would like to take the control for a few moments. It was an opportunity not to be missed, and having dipped a few degrees and back up again, that was it after perhaps half a minute. On getting home and recounting the trip to Sally and the boys, I was brought down to earth by our youngest exclaiming horror at the thought of me, even for a few seconds at the controls of a submarine, for after all as he pointed out, I couldn't even use the soda stream properly.

I suppose the defining period of my time in the House, was the miner's strike of 1984/5. Whilst the previous Labour government had closed many pits, the Heath Government had been defeated by the miners on this issue in 1974. Again in 1981 the Thatcher government had to give way to NUM demands, but plans were laid to ensure that they could never again hold an elected Government and the Country hostage. When the crunch came in March 1984, stocks were high and the summer was in front of us. In breach of the NUM rules, Arthur Scargill effectively called a national strike without a ballot. The Nottinghamshire miners voted by 20,000 to 7,000 not to strike, and faced massive intimidation from those who wished to ignore that vote, plus the physical pressure from the Yorkshire miners who "invaded" the County to try to force the strike onto unwilling Nottingham miners. As a result the Nottinghamshire miners created the Union of Democratic Miners, under Roy Lynch, and far from being scabs, they were simply following the right of any group of workers, to vote to strike or not as they choose, and not to have a strike forced upon them, in this case by a Union Leader with a political agenda rather than the interests of his members.

Very early one Monday morning during the first few weeks of the strike, I watched a news clip on TV showing the Labour member for Gorton, Gerald Kaufman, brandishing a very thick file of what he claimed was evidence of agent provocateur activity, and not trouble caused by striking miners. I rang the Chief Constable's office and was granted a meeting, to which two other senior offices attended, and I was able to take back to the Home Office a tape absolutely disputing Kaufman's claims. That day during a debate on the strike, Kaufman slammed the file on the dispatch box, to support his case. He refused to give way to me, perhaps because he knew I came from Nottinghamshire, and realised I would have challenged his theatrics, for to this day I believe that most, of not all, the pages in that thick file were just plain paper.

I travelled by car to Westminster each Monday morning, returning either on the Thursday evening, or Friday afternoon after the morning session in the House. I always stopped to check with the police who as a result of outside flying pickets, manned the roundabout on the M1, and to check the size of the coal store at the Radcliffe on Soar power station. There were many incidents of intimidation, and one that highlighted how vicious it became, was when a miner left his home to go to work, he was met on the doorstep by strikers who said. "Going into work; are the wife and family still at home?" Faced with that silent threat, the miner turned back into his house. Another was where the local union convenor had held a ballot, and having established that the vast majority voted not to strike supported his members who returned to work. For his refusal to ignore the wishes of his members, his car and home were covered in paint by strikers who clearly were not interested in the wishes of the majority. The bitterness between NUM and UDM members lasted for years after the strike ended, and even now there are those who were NUM supporters, who will have nothing to do with a UDM member. I do not claim that we handled the question of pit closures as well as we might, but that many had to close was inevitable. It was claimed that our deep mines produced cheap coal, but in truth we could buy coal from overseas at a fraction of the cost, and that the insistence on the use of British coal simply meant that the cost of generating electricity, was prohibitively high and was undermining British Industry as well as costing the domestic consumer much more than it should. It was also true that unpopular open cast coal could be produced at about a third of the cost from deep mines. At the time the average deep mined coal was roughly around £45 per tonne, opencast at £15 per tonne, yet some mines were being kept open costing over £100 per tonne. It could not go on like that, and had the NUM been prepared to face up to the economic truth and how it adversely affected the whole country, the wind-down could have been managed with much greater sympathy and far less human misery. However right or justified our attitude to the mines, politically in the East Midlands it was a disaster, and followed by the Poll Tax, our County of Nottinghamshire lost six of the seats it had held in 1983.

Whilst no-one could take pleasure from the obvious pain and hardship to many hundreds of people, there were incidences causing amusement. At junction 24 the centre of the roundabout was covered in dense undergrowth, and the police had noted a young lad regularly crossing the carriageway and disappearing into the cover. After a couple of weeks their curiosity got the better of them, and they found the lad had been growing cannabis under cover of the trees! The pickets who had managed to get through to the power station, foolishly picketed the front entrance not realising that the coal came by rail to the rear of the power station.

The Poll Tax was the final nail in any political hopes of survival that I might have had. It wasn't the concept that was wrong, for it was reasonable to ask that everyone who relied on, or used local services, should at least pay something towards those services. No Party at the time believed the old rating system could be sustained, and it militated against home owners improving their properties, for fear of being up-rated. I represented families in a pair of semi-detached homes, one of which had been up-rated in the mid seventies, and the adjacent home which made their improvements after that re-evaluation. These two identical homes found themselves paying very different rates. To compound the injustice, the higher rated home was occupied by a single old lady, whilst the lower rated home was occupied by a family of four.

Sadly I can only assume that the designers of the Poll Tax, - woops,sorry, the Community Charge - had never had any practical experience of Local Government, and were naïve to assume that the majority of Local Authorities, which were Labour controlled at that time, would not use every device to wreck the scheme. I had 22,000 Council properties in my constituency, and they had been accustomed to paying their rent along with their water rates, general rates, and in some cases their heating costs, on a fortnightly basis. For each member of a household to be faced with a booklet with ten vouchers equivalent to ten monthly payments, or two vouchers if they were going to pay in two half year instalments, or just one if they were to pay in one lump sum, was never going to work. It also meant that the other costs would require a separate method of collection from the head of the household.

A small delegation of members with years of experience of local government finance, met with the Minister on the basis that we approved the principle, but were certain that the planned method of implementation was bound to fail. There was a rule that if an individual had not used the "monthly" vouchers after the first three months of the year, they would have to pay in two six monthly instalments. Given that some authorities delayed sending out the books of vouchers, the subsequent queues of "Can't pay, won't pay" outside the magistrates courts was the inevitable consequence of not having thought through the practicalities of the collection of the tax. Added to the administrative problems, the attitude of those Authorities who had perhaps three years to go before they faced re-election, could boost the individual charge in that first year, giving them a war chest to spend on favoured topics and to fight the next election, was ignored. In Nottinghamshire's case the individual charge was boosted by over £100 per person, raising revenue they did not need, and in so doing brought odium solely down on our government who took the full blame for the tax that was more than double the original estimation.

That debacle led to the challenge to Mrs Thatcher's leadership. There had been a stalking horse the year before, but the Poll Tax and the European issue brought the situation to a head, and for me it became the worst two weeks of my Parliamentary career. My head told me that Mrs T should have retired with all honour after ten years in office, but I knew I owed her my chance to be a Member of Parliament. So my heart was with her, but when Geoffrey Howe made his famous resignation speech, one we were given to understand his good lady had taken years to write, and Geoffrey five minutes to a read, an election was inevitable. It was also clear that if Michael Heseltine didn't throw his hat in the ring, he never would.

We had never rejected a Prime Minister whilst in office, and I felt I should consult my members and we sent out some 700 letters seeking their views. I was pressured by some to make my view clear, but I took the view that it would have been insulting to members, to seek their view whilst at the same time telling them that I would vote this way or that, regardless of their opinions. The local BBC journalist tried hard to make me announce my view, but in the end accepted that I would wait until I'd gathered my member's views. She did indicate that I would get a call from the BBC on the Monday morning, before I left to drive to Westminster. I took the call, and happily did not recognise my interrogator. After a few questions were batted away, the voice said "surely you've nailed your colours to the mast." I agreed and said they were blue. End of interview. Only then did I realise I'd been talking to John Humphries, which was perhaps just as well. This was the same weekend of the first part of the TV series of Michael Dobbs' House of Cards. On arriving at the House, the chief whip Tim Renton, came across the member's lobby and congratulating me on how I'd handled the interview. In the light of the TV programme I could only reply "You may say that, I could not possibly comment!"

With John Major becoming prime Minister, David Waddington went to the Lords as leader of their House and as Lord privy Seal. Although the press had tipped me for some advancement, it was not to be, and David asked that I join him again as his PPS to seek to improve links between the two chambers. It also meant I remained with Lord Ferrers, who was delighted since he'd never had a PPS before. Attending at the bar of their Lordship's House for nearly two years, made me appreciate just what an excellent contribution it made to improving legislation. There was never an attempt to challenge the primacy of the Commons, and in practice, whatever amendments they made, unless the Commons agreed to those amendments, the view of the Lower House prevailed. It may not be logical, but it works, and I do fear that fiddling about with a full or part elected Upper Chamber, will have unintended consequences we will live to regret. I certainly doubt that many, if any, of the specialists that from time to time when appropriate to their skills, offer their advice from those red benches, will bother to seek election to an elected Upper House, and that expertise will be lost to our country.

There's little consolation in coming second even if it's just your first stab at getting elected, and less so when you've worked your socks off for nine years, granted doing what I genuinely loved. But it had been a great honour to have served Nottingham during those years, and I have nothing but grateful thanks to those who had given me the chance to stand, and the thousands that supported me through those years. Suffice to say I achieved more votes when I lost the seat, than when I'd won it in 1983. Funny business politics !

Once the political bug has bitten, it's very difficult to find a cure, and in my case I simply returned to Local Government, being elected to the County Council in 1993. I had one attempt at being an MEP in 1994, but that was the last year when MEPs were elected on a constituency basis, rather than the regional lists as was the case from 1999 onwards. That year first past the post did not operate in our favour and few of our Party succeeded.

Apart from returning to elected office at local level, I took on the role of speaker finder for the Millbank political supper club, which had been instrumental in my seeking and achieving a seat in the House of Commons. Whilst there, I persuaded a few colleagues to come and address the club, and having spoken to a number of constituencies had the chance to call in a few markers. Once back in the real world I was greatly helped by a good friend Patrick McLoughlin, now the Government Chief Whip, who found me, or twisted the arms of, two or three members from the Commons, to add to any MEPs or speakers from the Lords that made up a programme of five dinners each year. As a result, our chosen hotel gave us a really great deal,

With farmers in Leicestershire during a failed 1994 European Election bid

such that we had little difficulty in averaging fifty or more members and guests at our dinners spread through October to April each year. The club was a proving ground for many would be Councillors and MPs, and it's a proud recent record to have had Pauline Latham, Anna Soubry, Andy Stewart, John Hayes, Mark Spencer, Andrew Bridgen, who as members, made it to the Commons, as well as many others who attended simply as guests.

With Patrick's help, the quality of the MPs he sent us, greatly aided our aim of encouraging members and guests to stand for office either within the Party's administration, or as elected Councillors or Members of Parliament. Perhaps our, and his, greatest coup, was to send us two up and coming young newly elected Members of Parliament in David Cameron and George Osborne just prior to the 2005 General Election. It is true however that over the 50 years since the club's founding, our guests have covered just about every MP who has ever reached Cabinet level. The minute book makes great reading for any current guest, and given we've had 250 Dinners it would be invidious to pick out any of those guest speakers over those years.

I served on the County for sixteen years, and whilst it was clearly not as demanding or as rewarding as Westminster, I was grateful to those who selected me, and those who supported me over those four terms. Throughout those years we were in opposition, and it was frustrating in extreme to see one stupid decision after another taken by the majority Labour Group, based on dogma rather than any objective analysis. Never the less, just as I had as an MP, I derived great satisfaction in being able to achieve small benefits for my constituents, by knowing which door to bang on when something needed to be done.

I spent some time as shadow Education spokesman, clashing with the Labour Chairman Fred Riddell, who had made a name for himself Nationally as the most dyed in the wool stick in the mud, who would not address the fact that our County was either the last or one from last, each time the "league" table of County performances were published. His answer to that outcome was that Nottinghamshire was the most deprived County in the country, and that's why we did so badly in Education. Coming as I did from the East End of London, I refused to accept that as an excuse for failure. Most of his colleagues agreed with our group's criticisms, but not one of them would take on the Chairman. His, and the labour Group's first act on taking control in 1981 was to scrap plans to assist any bright children we'd identified in our schools, on the basis that Special Needs only applied to those at the bottom of the educational scale needing remedial help in reading and writing.

Such was his grip on all educational matters in the County, that when I was invited to meet the board of governors at a secondary school in my constituency, I was met by two officers of the council advising the board. The governors were concerned that year after year they had applied to have their temporary classrooms replaced with proper buildings. They had been told that it was all the fault of Kenneth Clarke who was Secretary of State at that time, and that he had blocked their requests. Before the meeting started I was called to the telephone to be berated by Fred Riddell firstly for visiting a school without his permission, and secondly he was not going to have me giving the governors false information as to how the capital grants were shared out throughout the County. I slammed the phone down on him, and to cut a long story short, the officers had to admit to the governors that the County, not Kenneth Clarke, decided priorities, and that in any case Fred would allocate any grant money elsewhere in the County and not to their school.

When the City separated from the County following local government reorganisation in the late 90s, Fred tried to move to find a City seat, but even the City Labour Party could not face having Fred as a colleague, and he decided to retire. As is the custom, there were the usual tributes paid to him for his years of service and particularly to education, and I was faced with making for me the most hypocritical speech of my entire career in public life. I did however start with a comment my mother had impressed upon me, "if you can't say something nice about someone, don't say anything at all ". Having said that, and heard the sharp intake of breath from the assembled councillors, I did say that of course it did not apply on this occasion. I've lived to regret that hypocritical speech.

In my last eight years I served as deputy leader, and worked in tandem with Cllr Kay Cutts who was one of the hardest working Councillors I have ever met. Since 2009 she has become Leader of the Council, and in the face of criticism from the usual suspects, she has certainly turned the Council's finances round, saving millions whilst at the same time transferring large sums to front line services and away from backroom bureaucracy. It had taken twenty eight years for the Conservatives to win control of the County, and regretfully those who had benefited from the profligacy of those years, are unlikely to thank the Conservatives for restoring some sense of reality to Local Government provision. No one likes losing what they have taken for granted for years, and those who were engaged in non jobs, or jobsworths, can't wait for a return of a Labour administration who would be only too pleased to rebuild what they believe is their public sector support base.

When I retired in 2009, I was honoured to have been made an Honorary Alderman for services to Nottinghamshire. In 2012 the City of Nottingham granted me the same honour, so I have nothing but happy memories due to public service over a period of forty years.

CHAPTER 9

THE CLOSING YEARS.

F ollowing a reasonably successful business career of over thirty years, forty years of one form or another of elected political office, and a life time involved in sport, it is time to reflect on and enjoy our closing years.

Politics is a form of incurable disease, for though retired from elected office in 2009, I still get occasionally rolled out to meet a request from some senior member of the Party to assist or advise on some problem or another. It's not too demanding, and it gave you a false sense that you haven't been forgotten and are still of some use. Our local Radio Nottingham call on me every couple of months to go on their early Monday morning phone-in knowing that without the constraints of office I can say just what I think, and so far I've not suffered any threats as a result. Equally when I hear or read of some, what to me seems an outrageous political plan, I send off a short "outraged of Barton in Fabis" to the press, and sometimes even now they print it!

As National Vice President and a non voting member of the National Council of British Rowing, I regularly attend their meetings just to keep up to scratch and know how things are progressing, and enjoy the privilege of attending such functions as the International Dinner, which each year celebrates the ever increasing success of our athletes. I've long since surrendered both my International and National Umpires licences, but still enjoy driving the launches at Holme Pierrepont regattas, trying not to tell the umpires how to do their job !

Perhaps the best recall of these years will always be the

outstanding performance of our athletes at the London Olympics. Attending the racing at Dorney Lake, and cheering on the extraordinary performance of our team, was an experience Sally and I will never forget. We attended two of the finals days, to witness the first GOLD to be won by any sport in the games, and to cheer and sympathise with the National Eight which had to be content with a BRONZE. The second attendance was to see at long last a much deserved GOLD medal for Katherine Grainger and her partner Anna Watkins in the womens double sculls. Granted there were around thirty thousand people there, including perhaps twenty five thousand Brits, I have never heard cheering like it, and the emotion engendered in the singing of the National Anthem was just something very special indeed.

On the two days we could not get to Dorney, we joined other members at Leander club at Henley, and watched the racing on the big screen. As the medals rolled in, the excitement at the club was tremendous, the champagne popped and a good time was had by all. It was just as well our cottage was just five minutes stagger from the club!

2010 was a year of first joy and then almost total disaster. After a wait of forty seven years, our club, the Nottingham and Union Rowing Club again won the Wyfold Cup at Henley Royal Regatta. Celebrations and partying all round. Within a few weeks I was diagnosed with cancer, and after a first minor operation, I returned home and was there in time to save Sally who without any warning collapsed with a brain haemorrhage, and got her to hospital for operations that undoubtedly saved her life. With surgery followed by rehabilitation lasting some eighteen weeks, Sally's hospitalisation overlapped my having two more operations, and at one time we were both in intensive care, and both nearly falling off the perch. We were both back home for Christmas that year, so whilst it was a year to forget, we were both back on our feet and enjoying life again.

The one big downside of both our operations was that we have had to come to terms with having to sell our large rambling old farmhouse for something more suitable to our age and limitations. So when coming up to my eightieth, we organised a party, and on the 25th of March some fifty friends and family gathered at Barton for what turned out to be a day to match anything the best of summers could have provided. A very good friend OI Lin provided a Chinese banquet with so much gorgeous food that even though most went round twice or three times, we were still able to provide everyone with a large takeaway ! I did try a sales job on the house, but no luck for our guests were all very happy with where they currently lived.

Recognising the old adage that the only certainties in life are Taxes and Death, we hope to have a few more years together, for now its forty eight years and counting.

Rowing Against the Tide